KENNETH BAKER, S.J.

THE WILL OF GOD

Finding and Fulfilling
Your Purpose in Life

IGNATIUS PRESS   SAN FRANCISCO

Cover art:
gettyimages.com/Larry Landolfi

Cover design by Riz Boncan Marsella

© 2012 by Ignatius Press, San Francisco
All rights reserved
ISBN 978-1-58617-707-2
Library of Congress Control Number 2012936917
Printed in the United States of America ∞

CONTENTS

INTRODUCTION

Why did God create me? The *Baltimore Catechism*'s answer is very profound: "God created me to know him, to love him, to serve him in this life and to be happy with him forever in the next life." There you have the answer to the question of human existence. Many of our contemporaries do not know that answer. Many spend their lives in a pointless search for pleasure and wealth. All of that is terminated by death, which comes to all, and many die in a state of despair. The modern solution, now legal in some states, is to provide them with physician-assisted suicide.

Where then is the meaning of life to be found? The stimulus for offering the reflections in this book is the fact that all the saints of the Church—while differing in personality and spirituality—have one thing in common: they all sought to do the will of God in their lives. I have been a Jesuit for over sixty years, and during that time I have read many lives of saints. What has struck me in all of them is the fact that each and every one sought to find the will of God in his life and then to do it to the best of his ability, in imitation of Jesus Christ, our Lord.

There are many levels or degrees of doing the will of God—going all the way from just avoiding mortal sin, to total dedication to doing God's will and serving him twenty-four hours of each day. The highest level is called the "mystical marriage", in which the individual is in conscious union with God in love during every waking moment. Many saints, like Teresa of Avila, after much effort attained this level.

Another aspect of doing God's will is the difference between man and the non-personal things of nature. By that I mean that elements, plants, animals, and heavenly bodies like the earth and the sun have a fixed nature. They do what they do necessarily. In the material universe only man is free and can choose to do this or that. All subhuman realities strive for their end by the necessity of their nature. They glorify God by being what they are and they do it necessarily. Man, however, freely strives for his end, namely, union with God for all eternity. This means that he can either embrace God's will or reject it. If he freely embraces it, he will be relatively happy in this life and have the hope of eternal happiness; if he rejects it and chooses some other end in life, such as pleasure or money or power, he will not achieve true happiness in this life, and he will not attain eternal happiness. Here we encounter the mystery of freedom.

Some excellent books on the importance of doing God's will, to mention just a few, are *The Love of God* by Saint Francis de Sales, *Self-Abandonment to Divine Providence* by J. P. de Caussade, S.J., and *My Father's Will* by Francis McGarrigle, S.J. In putting together these thoughts on God's will I have consulted these books. My goal is to provide the modern reader with a brief treatment of the wisdom of the Church on how to reach spiritual perfection, holiness, and intimacy with God by bringing one's life in all respects into conformity with the will of God.

The title *The Will of God* is inspired by the third petition of the Our Father, "Thy will be done on earth as it is in heaven." We will investigate the meaning of "will"—both the human will and the divine will. It is very important to know what God's will is and where we can find it. But knowing God's will is not the same thing as doing it. That is the rub. In order to achieve my purpose as a human being, in order to become a saint, it is not sufficient to know the will of God. After one knows the will of God, one must do it, embrace it, identify with it, and make it one's own. Those who do that imitate Saint Paul when he said, "[I]t is no longer I who live, but Christ who lives in me" (Gal 2:20).

It is crucial for each person to find out what God's will is for him in the particular circumstances in which he finds himself. That is not always easy to do. A goal of this book is to help individuals discover what God's will is for them—both in general, as regards all human beings, especially Catholics, and also in the particular circumstances of each person's life. Thus, if I keep the commandments and practice love of God and neighbor, what in particular is God calling me to do with my life? It is here that one must reflect on the duties of one's state in life—married, single, priest, religious, parent, child, student, teacher, employer, employee, and so forth. God calls each one in a different way because each person is unique and the divine grace he gives to each one is different.

It is one thing to know God's will for oneself, but it is something different to actually do it. For most of us, it is perhaps easier to know God's will than it is to accomplish it perfectly. So here we will consider not just God's will in an objective sense but also the practical problem of how to carry it out and do it in daily life. The invocation "thy will be done" in the Our Father stresses the point of doing God's will—that is the object of "be done".

My hope and prayer is that this little book will help its readers to find God's will in their lives and to embrace it according to the grace God gives them. The result will surely be charity, joy, peace, patience, kindness, goodness, fidelity, constancy, and eventually, happiness with God forever in heaven.

I

Sanctity and the Will of God

Blessed are those whose way is blameless,
   who walk in the *law* of the LORD!
Blessed are those who keep his *testimonies*,
   who seek him with their whole heart,
who also do no wrong,
   but walk in his ways!
You have commanded your *precepts*
   to be kept diligently.
O that my ways may be steadfast
   in keeping your *statutes*!
Then I shall not be put to shame,
   having my eyes fixed on all your *commandments*.
I will praise you with an upright heart,
   when I learn your righteous *ordinances*.
I will observe your *statutes*;
   O forsake me not utterly!

—Psalm 119:1–8 I (*Aleph*); italics added here and hereafter[1]

"For this is the will of God, your sanctification" (1 Thess 4:3). Saint Paul tells us in clear language that the will of God is our sanctification or holiness. God in himself is

[1] See end of this chapter, pages 17–18, for Greek alphabet explanation.

absolute holiness, the fullness of sanctity. The closer we unite ourselves to him and the more we become like him, to that extent we also grow in holiness. Holiness is another word for perfection. God is infinite perfection, so as we become more perfect, we become more like God. It is the will of Jesus that we become perfect like our heavenly Father, for he says in Matthew 5:48, "You, therefore, must be perfect, as your heavenly Father is perfect." That is a lifetime task since, as limited human beings, we can never attain the perfection of the Father, but we can strive for it and improve each day if we make use of the gifts that God gives, both in the natural order and in the supernatural order. We grow in faith, hope, and love, but we can never have too much of these virtues. We can never reach a limit and be able to say, "I don't need any more faith, hope, and love."

The perfection Jesus recommends to us is meant for all, not just for priests, nuns, and religious. That command to become perfect occurs in the Sermon on the Mount, which was addressed to a large crowd, not just to his close disciples. So it also includes all members of the Church, both lay and religious.

What is sanctity? It is a union in love with God; it is conformity with God's will in all things. It is putting into practice the prayer of Jesus in his agony in the Garden of Gethsemane when he said to his heavenly Father, "[N]ot my will, but yours, be done" (Lk 22:42).

How do I find God's will in my life so that I can do it and strive for the perfection that God wants me to have? On this point theologians like J. P. de Caussade, S.J., make a distinction between God's active will and his passive will.[2]

God's active will—Saint Thomas calls it God's "will of expression" (*voluntas signi*)—is contained in his positive commands. These include such things as the Ten Commandments, the evangelical counsels, the teaching of the Church, and just civil laws; it also includes the circumstances of my life, such as my family, the time of my birth, my gender, my physical and mental talents, and so forth. These aspects of my life are directly and actively willed by God; otherwise, they would never have happened and I would either be someone else or not exist. Obedience to God's will of expression is the normal or usual way of attaining perfection.

God's passive will means accepting with patience, love, and gratitude everything that happens to me in my daily life—sickness and health, joy and sorrow, friendship with others and rejection, and so forth. Saint Thomas calls this aspect of God's will his "will of good pleasure" (*voluntas beneplaciti*). All of these things are aspects of divine providence, which is God's plan for the world and also for me as an individual. That plan has been known by God from all eternity, but it is put into effect by his will to create the world and to govern it by his omnipotent power.

It is one thing to know God's will and another thing to do it or to submit oneself to it. It should be noted

[2] J. P. de Caussade, S.J., *Self-Abandonment to Divine Providence* (Rockford, Ill.: Tan Books, 1987), pp. 5–8.

that all natural things do God's will *necessarily* according to the nature that God has given to each individual thing. So elements, minerals, plants, and animals do God's will just by being what they are. Natural laws govern each entity and they are not free to change. So a dog cannot change himself into a horse. Each thing operates therefore according to its nature.

Man is different from everything else in the material universe because he alone has free will and can determine himself to his end. Natural, impersonal things have their end set for them by the Creator. Man's end is to serve God freely and eventually to attain the face-to-face vision of God in heaven after his death.

An essential aspect of man's being is his mortality. Every human person from Adam and Eve to the present has died; there is no escape and no exception. The problem of death and personal survival after death is a crucial question for each one of us. Each person must confront the question: Why do I exist? Where did I come from, since I came into existence years ago and did not create myself? What is my final destiny? How should I live my life? As Christians we know, from the revelation of Jesus Christ and the infallible teaching of the Church, that our God is a God of love and that he created us out of his goodness; he has given us a supernatural destiny, namely, to be united to him in knowledge and love in heaven for all eternity if we follow his will and his commandments.

The Bible says that the average life span of man is seventy years—and eighty years for those who are strong (Ps 90:10). God gives us that time to work out our salvation in fear and trembling. Our final destiny for all eternity, since we possess an immortal soul, is either heaven or hell. Those who do God's will and keep his commandments will be saved and will be happy. They attain the end for which God created them. Those who reject God's will and flout his commandments will be lost and will be miserable for all eternity. That is a truth to be meditated on frequently.

In order to carry out God's will in my life at all times it is helpful to realize that God is present to me and sees me 24/7. Since God is everywhere, there is no place where I can hide from him so that he does not know what I am doing. Just as a fish is surrounded by water and the bird is surrounded by the air, so also I am surrounded by God at all times. Speaking to the skeptical Greeks in Athens, Saint Paul said with regard to the true God, "Yet he is not far from each one of us, for 'In him we live and move and have our being'" (Acts 17:27–28).

Since God as absolute being is the source of all existence and therefore keeps everything in existence, it follows that he must be everywhere. He keeps every atom and every element in my body and in the universe in existence. If he were to forget anything, it would cease to exist. This reflection helps me to realize that God is present to me at every moment of my life. He created me because he loves me and wants me to be happy with him forever. Being aware of God's presence is a strong motive not to displease him by going against his will. If by human weakness we should fail in some way to follow his law, we can always repent, tell him we are sorry, and go to confession at the first opportunity. And because of our baptism and the possession of sanctifying grace, the Holy Trinity dwells within us, as Jesus says: "If a man loves me, he will keep my word, and my Father will love him, and we will come to him and make our home with him" (Jn 14:23).

To give meaning to my life, it is essential to know God's will—to know what he expects of me. I learn that from my parents, from the Bible, from the *Catechism* and from the teaching of the Church. But it is one thing to know what the will of God is and something else to actually do it and conform myself to the will of God. The most important thing is to do the will of God. The learned priest who knows the will of God but does not follow it is in a much worse situation than the uneducated grandmother who prays fervently, keeps the commandments, and practices the love of God and neighbor.

Spiritual writers speak of three "ways" or levels of the spiritual life: *purgative, illuminative,* and *unitive.* In the purgative way, the soul is first cleansed of all mortal sins and attachment to mortal sin. In the illuminative way, one strives for greater holiness by avoiding all deliberate venial sins. The highest level is the unitive way. At this level the soul is so purified from all opposition to the will of God that it avoids all deliberate imperfections, determined to do whatever is most pleasing to God and to imitate Jesus by accepting and embracing whatever joy or sorrow he may be pleased to send.[3]

We see marvelous examples of the unitive way in the lives of the saints, especially those who have written down their experience of God. Good examples of this are Saint Teresa of Avila, Saint John of the Cross, Saint Francis de Sales, Saint John de Brebeuf, and many others.

Saint Ignatius of Loyola, founder of the Jesuit order, gives expression to the unitive way in his famous prayer called the "*Suscipe*" in his little book on how to make a retreat, *Spiritual Exercises*:

> Take, O Lord, and receive all my liberty, my memory, my understanding, and my entire will, all that I have and possess. Thou hast given all to me. To Thee, O Lord, I return it. All is Thine, dispose of it wholly according to Thy Will. Give me Thy love and Thy grace, for this is sufficient for me.[4]

Please note the quote from Psalm 119 at the beginning of this chapter. Each chapter will begin with a stanza from this psalm. Psalm 119 is the longest psalm, containing 176 verses. It is artistically composed. There are twenty-two letters in the Hebrew alphabet. This psalm contains twenty-two stanzas of eight verses each,

---

[3] Francis J. McGarrigle, S.J., *My Father's Will* (Milwaukee, Wis.: The Bruce Publishing Co., 1944), p. 203.

[4] Louis J. Puhl, S.J., *The Spiritual Exercises of St. Ignatius* (Chicago: Loyola Press, 1952), no. 102.

for a total of 176 verses. All eight verses in each stanza begin with the same letter of the Hebrew alphabet. So the first eight verses above all begin with the letter *A* (*Aleph*); the next eight begin with *B* (*Beth*), and so forth.

Each verse is praise for God's law and his commands, which are expressions of his will. Eight synonyms for God's will are used, and most of them occur in each stanza. They are *law, word, testimony, ordinance, promise, decree, precept,* and *commandment.* This is a beautiful and powerful psalm. It is reported of Blaise Pascal, the famous French mathematician and philosopher, that he prayed this psalm every day. Since we are reflecting on the will of God, it is helpful to remind ourselves of what the Bible says about it in Psalm 119.

2

Human Will

How can a young man keep his way pure?
    By guarding it according to your *word*.
With my whole heart I seek you;
    let me not wander from your *commandments*!
I have laid up your *word* in my heart,
    that I might not sin against you.
Blessed are you, O LORD;
    teach me your *statutes*!
With my lips I declare
    all the *ordinances* of your mouth.
In the way of your *testimonies* I delight
    as much as in all riches.
I will meditate on your *precepts*,
    and fix my eyes on your ways.
I will delight in your *statutes*;
    I will not forget your *word*.

—Psalm 119:9–16 II (*Beth*)

Man is endowed with a will because he is a spiritual
being composed of body and soul. The basic meaning of "will" is that it is an intellectual appetite. An
appetite is a power of the soul that responds to a per-
ceived good. Since man has both a body and a soul,

he has sense appetites, such as the desire for food, drink, clothing, and shelter, and he also has intellectual desires, such as the desire to know, to love, and to have friends. What we are concerned with here is man's intellectual appetite, which is called his "will".

There is an essential, mutual relationship between intellect and will. The intellect grasps or understands reality, real things existing outside of itself. All of his knowledge comes through the senses. The scholastics expressed this by saying: *There is nothing in the mind that is not first in the senses*. The intellect forms ideas of the things it knows. Ideas are mental images or representations of external reality. The main characteristic of intellect is that it grasps or perceives things under the aspect of being. The correspondence between the mind and reality is called "truth". All being is one, true, and good; these are known as the transcendentals of being.

The intellect perceives being as true and presents it, as it were, to the will. The will perceives reality under the aspect of the good. So the object of the will is goodness. The will affirms goodness and strives for or desires those good things that it sees as perfective of itself.

Because of the essential relationship between intellect and will, they are both powers of the one human person; intellect moves the will under one aspect, and the will moves the intellect under another aspect. The will can desire only what is known by the intellect, so the intellect presents the good to be desired to the will. But since the object of the will is the good, and the intellect is also a good thing or power, the will can move the intellect to think about this or that, or to stop thinking about one thing and to think about something else. So there is a mutual dependence between intellect and will.

An essential aspect of man's will is that it is free. Thus, we say that man has free will. When it comes to willing some concrete or particular reality, the will is not determined to choose one thing as opposed to another. For lunch on Monday, a boy might choose a hamburger and fries; on Tuesday, he might choose to have a hot dog and a milkshake. This truth about the will can be expressed briefly: the will can choose between opposites. It is not determined to one thing. All natural things, like minerals, plants, and animals, have a nature that determines them to act in a certain way. A dog is a dog and a pig is a pig; oxygen and hydrogen always act in the same way. The sun rises in the east and sets in the west. Only man, among all earthly or material beings, is not determined to act in one way. Since he has a rational appetite, which we call "will", he enjoys free will. It is his intellect and will that make him be in the image and likeness of God, since God is infinite knowing and willing.

The purpose of this book is to investigate and reflect on the will of God, since we pray in the Our Father, "Thy will be done on earth as it is in heaven." In order to understand something about the will of God, it is necessary to have some idea of what is meant by "will" as such. God's will is infinitely superior to man's will, but there is a similarity between the two, since God is infinite Spirit and man is a finite spirit and intellect and will are essential components of spirit.

For our purpose here it is important to note that the will *commands* the intellect to do certain things. The will, therefore, is an agent in reference to the intellect. What moves the will to act is the good as an end to be achieved or affirmed. When we pray, "Thy will be done", we are referring to the commands given by the divine will. Saint Thomas Aquinas refers to this as his "will of expression", which, for example, is found in the Ten Commandments in the revelation given to Moses on Mount Sinai.

As the Creator of the whole universe, God has given each thing its own nature, which determines the type of being it is. As we read in the book of Wisdom: "[Y]ou have arranged all things by measure and number and weight" (11:20). All things below man—the sun, the moon, the stars—are ruled by natural necessity. Man's nature is different. He alone has reason in the material universe (here we are not considering angels, who are pure spirits with intellect and will, but no body). Natural things obey God by the necessity of their nature. Man's nature is different. He rules himself by reason and God deals with each of his creatures according to the nature he gave to it. So God deals with man as a rational, free being. Man is guided in his activities by his reason and by natural law. The

Greek philosophers Socrates, Plato, and Aristotle worked out many of the details of the natural law.

Having considered the will and in particular the human will, we will now reflect on the divine will and how it is manifested in nature and in divine revelation in the history of Israel and in Jesus Christ, the Son of God.

3

Divine Will

Deal bountifully with your servant,
    that I may live and observe your *word*.
Open my eyes, that I may behold
    wondrous things out of your *law*.
I am a sojourner on earth;
    hide not your *commandments* from me!
My soul is consumed with longing
    for your *ordinances* at all times.
You rebuke the insolent, accursed ones,
    who wander from your *commandments*;
take away from me their scorn and contempt,
    for I have kept your *testimonies*.
Even though princes sit plotting against me,
    your servant will meditate on your *statutes*.
Your *testimonies* are my delight,
    they are my counselors.

—Psalm 119:17–24 III (*Gimel*)

Will and intellect go together. Will affirms and desires what the intellect perceives and presents to it. Since God is infinite intelligence, it follows that he is also infinite will. But since God is absolutely simple and absolute goodness, his will is identified with his goodness. So the act of willing in God is one of affirmation of himself, love of himself as supreme goodness. In confirmation of this Saint Thomas Aquinas says: "In every intellectual being there is will, just as in every sensible being there is animal appetite. And so there must be will in God, since there is intellect in Him. And as His intellect is His own existence, so is His will." [1] Also in God there is no real distinction between his will and the activity of his will, as there is in us, since he is absolutely simple, having no composition of any kind. As Saint Thomas says, his will is his existence.

Since the object of God's will is his own infinite existence and goodness, he is absolutely free with regard to all limited, created beings. Each one of them imitates God's own being in some limited way, and so is a particular good. God necessarily wills and loves himself, but he is under no necessity to create finite beings such as we find in the material universe because they are all particular goods. God loves all of the things he has made, but he loves them freely. In Genesis we read that God saw each thing he made as good: "And God saw everything that he had made, and behold, it was very good" (Gen 1:31).

There was a time in the past when the universe and the world did not exist. "In the beginning God created the heavens and the earth" (Gen 1:1). If we reflect and wonder about the existence of the sun, the moon,

---

[1] Thomas Aquinas, *Summa Theologica* I, 19, 1 (Westminster, Md.: Christian Classics, 1981). Hereafter abbreviated *STh*.

and the stars, if we wonder where we came from, since we all had a beginning in time, the answer is that God created us out of nothing; he made us out of nothing. God did that by an act of his will—he freely willed this universe into existence, and he freely willed me into existence. So his will, operating through his omnipotent power, is the cause or reason for my limited existence here and now.

God gave a nature or form to everything he created. He created the natural laws of cause and effect—every agent acts for an end—the law of gravity, the speed of light, and so forth. All of these effects are the result of his will—they reflect the will of God. As we have said, they do what they do necessarily, according to their nature. But man is different from everything else in the material universe because God created him with an intellect and a will. He is spiritual and free, and so he has his destiny in his own hands. Man conducts himself by reason. By reason he can discern what is good for him, and what is evil or harms him. Since he is free, man can choose and decide for himself how to act and how to deal with other human beings who are like him. So man governs himself, or should govern himself, by the natural law, which is a participation in the eternal law of God. In this way, on the natural level, God makes his will known to man. Plato and Aristotle made great advances for mankind in analyzing and writing down what it means to be a rational and free human being.

When we pray in the Our Father "thy will be done on earth as it is in heaven", we are referring to the expressions of the divine will. This important invocation does not refer to the will of God as it is in itself in the divine essence; it refers rather to what God wills with regard to me and the world. This is what Saint Thomas and other theologians refer to as the "will of expression" in God.[2] This means that God's will for man is expressed in five ways: *prohibition, precept, counsel, operation,* and *permission.*

God prohibits evil and commands good deeds to be done by his commandments; he counsels us to strive for perfection. Since he made man free, he permits him to commit evil. His operation means what he arranges for us in divine providence by the circumstances we find ourselves in, such as personal talents, sickness or health, time of birth, nationality, and so forth. This latter aspect of the divine will is also called his "will of good pleasure". We are counseled and urged to accept these things as manifestations of the will of God. In this regard Saint Thomas says:

> That precept, counsel, and prohibition are called the will of God is clear from the words of Matt. 6:10: *Thy will be done on earth as it is in heaven.* That permission and operation are called the will of God is clear from Augustine (*Enchir. 95*), who says: *Nothing is done, unless the Almighty wills it to be done, either by permitting it, or by actually doing it.*[3]

---

[2] *STh* I, 19, 11 and 12.
[3] *STh* I, 19, 12.

4

Revelation and the Will of God

My soul clings to the dust;
  revive me according to your *word*!
When I told of my ways, you answered me;
  teach me your *statutes*!
Make me understand the way of your *precepts*,
  and I will meditate on your wondrous *works*.
My soul melts away for sorrow;
  strengthen me according to your *word*!
Put false ways far from me;
  and graciously teach me your *law*!
I have chosen the way of faithfulness,
  I set your *ordinances* before me.
I cleave to your *testimonies*, O LORD;
  let me not be put to shame!
I will run in the way of your *commandments*
  when you enlarge my understanding!

—Psalm 119:25–32 IV (*Dalet*)

Catholics believe that the Bible is a holy book because it contains divine revelation, that is, God's words and deeds concerning his nature and his will with regard to man and the universe. The English word "revelation" is derived from the Latin *revelare*, which means "to unveil or disclose something". It often means a sudden and unexpected communication of important knowledge that profoundly affects the life of the recipient. That is certainly true of the profound revelation contained in the Bible.

According to the Bible, revelation comes primarily through the word of God. In fact, some theologians hold that the Bible has a quasi-sacramental character because the one who hears or reads it receives grace to enter into a deeper relationship with God.[1] Jesus Christ, as the Incarnate Word of God, is the revelation of God in Person. Because Jesus is the Word of God in the flesh, every word and deed of his is a revelation to us. The object of that revelation is God himself and his will with regard to man and his future.

Divine revelation means that God makes known to us truths concerning his own nature, such as three Persons in one God, and also his plan or purpose in the creation of the world and in the creation of mankind.

Man can know by natural reason certain things about God, such as his existence, his goodness, and his omnipotent power (see Rom 1:18–20). But reason itself cannot know that man is destined to a supernatural end, that he is destined for the face-to-face vision of God in heaven for all eternity. Such a purpose for man is beyond his nature. But it is a fact

---

[1] See *New Catholic Encyclopedia*, (1967), vol. 12, s.v. "Revelation, Theology of".

that God has raised man to the supernatural level and has revealed his purpose to him. This means that he has an end that is above and beyond the requirements of his nature.

Before his sin, Adam, the first man and the father of the human race, enjoyed a friendly relation with God. After his sin, God promised him that he would send a savior in the future (Gen 3:15), but Adam was expelled from Paradise and lost his preternatural gifts, such as integrity and immortality.

Salvation history begins with the call of Abraham as recorded in the book of Genesis. God also raised up Isaac, Jacob, Joseph, and Moses, as we read in the dramatic development and history of Israel, the people chosen by God to receive his revelation and to be the source of the Messiah and Redeemer of the whole human race. God revealed himself to them and manifested to them his will. A climax was reached by his miraculous liberation of the Israelites from the land of Egypt and then his making of the covenant with Moses and Israel on Mount Sinai. During the forty years of wandering in the wilderness the Israelites were forged into a recognizable people with a covenant, a law, and a leader in Moses. Through his covenant and his law God revealed to Israel his will regarding how they should worship him, the true God, and how they should live as a people. He gave them the Ten Commandments on how to live, and the liturgical rules in the book of Leviticus on how to show proper worship for God. All of this foreshadowed the future and definitive revelation that would be made known by Jesus, the Messiah.

After the Israelites miraculously crossed the Jordan River and entered into the Promised Land, the chosen people gradually became an organized civil society under King Saul and, especially, King David. God spoke through the prophets and guided Israel in the persons of Samuel, Amos, Isaiah, Jeremiah, Ezekiel, Daniel, and the other prophets. That is all written down and recorded in the Old Testament. All of this was preparatory to the coming of the Messiah, since everything in the Old Testament refers to the Messiah in one way or another. Adam, Abraham, Moses, David, and the prophets are types of the Messiah who was to come, namely, Jesus Christ, who was born of the Virgin Mary in Bethlehem of Judea over two thousand years ago. Saint Augustine put it well when he said that the New Testament is hidden in the Old and the Old Testament is made manifest in the New.[2] The fullness of revelation is found in Jesus Christ, who is both God and man. So he not only revealed to us God's plan, his will for creation and mankind, but he is that revelation in his Person. He proved his claim to be God by his life, his teaching, his miracles, his Passion, his death, and his Resurrection.

On Peter and the other apostles Jesus established his Church and sent them into the whole world to

---

[2] See Vatican II, Dogmatic Constitution on Divine Revelation, *Dei Verbum* (1965), no. 16.

preach the gospel and to administer the sacraments, for the sanctification and the salvation of all mankind (Mt 28:18–20). The Magisterium of the Catholic Church preserves, explains, and protects the divine revelation contained in the Bible and in Tradition. She is the only authentic interpreter of the Bible and revelation. On the role of the Magisterium the Council said: "Yet this Magisterium is not superior to the word of God, but is its servant. It teaches only what has been handed on to it. At the divine command and with the help of the Holy Spirit, it listens to this devoutly, guards it with dedication and expounds it faithfully. All that it proposes for belief as being divinely revealed is drawn from this single deposit of faith." [3]

From what has just been said, it should be clear what revelation is, where it can be found, and who guards and interprets it. A further point is the content of revelation. What does it tell us about God, the world, and my own personal existence?

Vatican II in its document on divine revelation (*Dei Verbum*) answers these questions clearly and succinctly: "It pleased God in his goodness and wisdom, to reveal himself and to make known the mystery of his will. His will was that men should have access to the Father through Christ, the Word made flesh, in the Holy Spirit, and thus become sharers in the divine nature." [4] So revelation has to do with salvation, with

---

[3] *Dei Verbum*, no. 10; see also nos. 11–13.
[4] Ibid., no. 2.

doing God's will in this life, and with man's future in the next life. We have "access to the Father" and "become sharers in the divine nature" by faith in Jesus Christ and by living according to his commandment of love of God and neighbor.

It is clear from the study of the Bible that God revealed himself to man by gradually communicating the mystery of himself in words and deeds. His deeds manifest his almighty power and his love for man; the words explain the meaning of the deeds. This is true of God's great miracles in the Old Testament and also of the birth, life, miracles, death, and Resurrection of Jesus in the New Testament. The four Gospels give a historical account of the main points in the life of Jesus. They tell us what he said and what he did and the impact he made on those who heard him and associated with him.

Concerning revelation and God's will, Vatican II said: "It pleased God, in his goodness and wisdom, to reveal himself and to make known the mystery of his will (cf. Eph. 1:9). His will was that man should have access to the Father, through Christ, the Word made flesh." Again the Council said in the same document: "By divine revelation God wished to manifest and communicate both himself and the eternal decrees of his will concerning the salvation of mankind." [5]

The meaning and importance of revelation with regard to the triune nature of God and his will for

[5] Ibid., nos. 2, 6.

man is clearly expressed in the Dogmatic Constitution on Divine Revelation of the Second Vatican
Council (*Dei Verbum*). The document can be read eas-
ily in less than an hour and is highly recommended
for those who wish to pursue this subject in more
detail.

5

The Will of God in the Old Testament

Teach me, O LORD, the way of your *statutes*;
  and I will keep it to the end.
Give me understanding, that I may keep your *law*
  and observe it with my whole heart.
Lead me in the path of your *commandments*,
  for I delight in it.
Incline my heart to your *testimonies*,
  and not to gain!
Turn my eyes from looking at vanities;
  and give me life in your *ways*.
Confirm to your servant your *promise*,
  which is for those who fear you.
Turn away the reproach which I dread;
  for your *ordinances* are good.
Behold, I long for your *precepts*;
  in your righteousness give me life!

—Psalm 119:33–40 V (*Hey*)

One of the main themes in the Old Testament is
that the man who obeys God's law, who keeps his
commandments, who does his will, will be blessed
by God. The faithful servant is rewarded with a long
life, like Methuselah, or with many descendants and

35

possessions, as in the case of Abraham, Jacob, and David. Those who sin against God's law are punished, like Adam and Eve, who were expelled from the Garden of Eden and condemned to die. Moses was not permitted to enter the Promised Land because of one fault, and David was punished for his adultery with Bathsheba.

It is stated often that the man who does God's will and obeys his law will be blessed. This truth is stated in the very first psalm, in the first two verses: "Blessed is the man who walks not in the counsel of the wicked . . . but his delight is in the law of the LORD" (Ps 1:1–2). Again, we read in Psalm 25:10: "All the paths of the LORD are mercy and faithfulness, for those who keep his covenant and his testimonies." We have already seen that God's law and will are praised in each of the 176 verses in Psalm 119, using eight synonyms for God's will: *law, word, testimony, ordinance, promise, decree, precept, and commandment.*

The sad story about the fall of Adam is familiar to all, even to non-Christians. God created Adam and Eve out of the dust of the earth. He endowed them with many gifts, both natural and supernatural. He put them in the Garden of Eden, filled with beauty and fruitful trees. There was only one prohibition: they were not to eat of the fruit of the tree of the knowledge of good and evil. Satan, in the form of a snake, tempted Eve and she fell; Eve in turn urged Adam to eat the fruit, and he did. As a result of this sin they were expelled from Paradise; they lost their special gifts of immortality and integrity and were doomed to die, to return to the dust from which they were taken. They acted against God's will—they committed a serious sin—and for that they were severely punished but not totally repudiated by God. He promised them a Savior, a son of the Woman, who would defeat Satan (see Gen 3:15).

Genesis 12–25 tells the story of Abraham, a just and humble man who was obedient to God's will in all things. He was even willing to sacrifice his only son, Isaac, in order to carry out God's will. This was a test of Abraham's faith and good will. At the last minute an angel stopped him, once it was clear that he would obey God in all things. As his reward, God promised him that he would be the father of many nations, especially of the chosen people, and that the Savior of the world, the Messiah, would be one of his descendants.

Another outstanding example of obedience to God's will is that of Moses. God blessed him and chose him to lead the Hebrews out of the slavery of Egypt and to take them to the Promised Land of Palestine. Moses was faithful in all things. God revealed to him from the burning bush his name, "I AM WHO I AM" (Ex 3:14). God made a covenant with Moses and the people on Mount Sinai. From this point on the refugees from Egypt are the favored, the chosen people of the Lord. To them he makes known his will in the Ten Commandments and how he is to be worshipped.

The warrior Joshua survived the forty years in the wilderness and was chosen by God to lead the people into the Promised Land after the death of Moses. After conquering the land, Joshua urges the people to be obedient to the covenant and to obey all of God's laws. The people reply, "The LORD our God we will serve, and his voice we will obey" (Josh 24:24).

Saul, the first king of Israel, who lived about 1050 B.C., is a tragic figure because he did not obey God's will. He was chosen by God, but when he disobeyed God's will by taking the booty from a vanquished city, he was rejected and replaced by the young David, a shepherd and son of Jesse (see 1 Sam).

David was a man after God's own heart. He was a faithful servant to Saul and won many battles for him. After the death of Saul he became king, and he was faithful to the covenant and promoted the worship of the true God. He was also a sinner because of his adultery with Bathsheba and the killing of her husband, Uriah. But he repented his sins and expressed his sorrow in the beautiful Psalm 51 (see also 1 and 2 Sam). God promised David that his kingdom would last forever and that the Messiah would be one of his descendants (2 Sam 7:11–17).

The 150 psalms are often called the "prayer book" of the Church. Priests pray them every day in the Divine Office. Many of the psalms, such as Psalm 119 mentioned above, praise the law of the Lord—his commands and his will. The basic idea is that blessed, just, and happy is the man who obeys God's law. The theme of Psalm 119 is summed up briefly in verse 97: "Oh, how I love your law! It is my meditation all the day."

A similar sentiment is expressed in Psalm 40:8: "I delight to do your will, O my God; your law is within my heart." Again we read in Psalm 143:10: "Teach me to do your will, for you are my God! Let your good spirit lead me on a level path!"

Probably written between 500 and 400 B.C., the book of Job is a profound reflection on the problem of evil, especially the suffering of the innocent, like little children and faithful worshippers of God. Job is innocent and declares his innocence. In spite of that, God allows Satan to test and torment him terribly. But in the midst of his intense suffering Job never blames God or curses him. He accepts his suffering and God's holy will, with patience, faith, and hope. He expresses his attitude toward God beautifully in Job 1:21–22: "Naked I came from my mother's womb, and naked shall I return; the LORD gave, and the LORD has taken away; blessed be the name of the LORD."

The idea of the happiness of the man who does the will of God is repeated in the wisdom books of the Old Testament—Proverbs, Tobit, Ecclesiastes, Sirach, and Wisdom. Tobit prays, "[God] now deal with me according to your pleasure", meaning according to God's will (Tob 3:6). The wise man in Proverbs says, "Many are the plans in the mind of a man, but it is the purpose of the LORD that will be established" (Prov 19:21).

In the second century B.C. the warrior Judas Maccabeus prayed, "It is better for us to die in battle than to see the misfortunes of our nation and of the

sanctuary. But as his will in heaven may be, so he
will do (1 Macc 3:59–60).

God's word in the Old Testament teaches us that
the person who obeys him and keeps his law will be
blessed in this life. In the early period before the Baby-
lonian Captivity in 587 B.C. the Israelites understood
this in a material way: a long life, children, and possessions, such as land and animals. Later, after suffering the destruction of Jerusalem by the Babylonians
and being taken into captivity in exile, the Israelites
began to accept the idea that, since many good people died young and the innocent suffered without
rewards in this life, God will reward those who love
him and keep his law with a happy life after death.
Thus, many Israelites were being prepared to accept
the revelation of Jesus about the kingdom of God and
eternal life with the Father, Son, and Holy Spirit for
those who have faith in Jesus, are baptized, and become
members of his community or Church. John the Baptist was part of that preparation, so after he was arrested,
"Jesus came into Galilee, preaching the gospel of God,
and saying, 'The time is fulfilled, and the kingdom of
God is at hand; repent, and believe in the gospel'"
(Mk 1:14–15).

6

The Will of God in the New Testament

Let your mercy come to me, O LORD,
   your salvation according to your *promise*;
then shall I have an answer for those who taunt me,
   for I trust in your *word*.
And take not the word of truth utterly out of my
      mouth
   for my hope is in your *ordinances*.
I will keep your *law* continually,
   for ever and ever;
and I shall walk at liberty,
   for I have sought your *precepts*.
I will also speak of your *testimonies* before kings,
   and shall not be put to shame;
for I find my delight in your *commandments*,
   which I love.
I revere your *commandments*, which I love,
   and I will meditate on your *statutes*.

—Psalm 119:41–48 VI (*Vau*)

Jesus Christ, Son of Man and Son of God, is the
supreme model or example of doing the will of God.
He fulfilled God's will perfectly from the first moment
of his existence in the womb of his virginal Mother.

The one human being who comes closest to imitating him is his Mother, who embraced God's will for her when she said to the angel Gabriel, "Behold, I am the handmaid of the Lord; let it be done unto me according to your word" (Lk 1:38). Her *fiat* anticipates the *fiat* in the Our Father, "Thy will be done" (*fiat voluntas tua*).

The very first words to come out of the mouth of the Child Jesus at the age of twelve, when his parents found him in the temple after an absence of three days, express concern for his Father's will. In response to his Mother's question about why he acted so, Jesus replied: "How is it that you sought me? Did you not know that I must be in my Father's house?" (Lk 2:49). The Greek text can also be translated, "Did you not know that I must be about my Father's business?"

When Jesus preached the gospel of the kingdom of God in his public life, he said many times that he had come into this world to do the will of his heavenly Father. And he tells his disciples and us to pray that the Father's will should be done when we pray the Our Father: "Thy will be done on earth as it is in heaven" (Mt 6:10).

Jesus says that in order to enter the kingdom of heaven it is necessary to do the will of God: "Not every one who says to me, 'Lord, Lord,' shall enter the kingdom of heaven, but he who does the will of my Father who is in heaven" (Mt 7:21).

When we reflect on the great love Jesus had for his Mother, it is amazing to see that he puts those who do the will of God on the same level as his mother. On one occasion, when he was busy preaching, she wanted to speak to him. In reply to the man who told him his mother was outside the house wanting to see him, he said: " 'Who is my mother, and who are my brethren?' And stretching out his hand toward his disciples, he said, 'Here are my mother and my brethren! For whoever does the will of my Father in heaven is my brother, and sister, and mother' " (Mt 12:46–50; see also Mk 3:31–35 and Lk 8:19–21).

In the Gospels Jesus says several times that he is not seeking his own will, but the will of his Father. In John 5:30 Jesus says: "I can do nothing on my own authority; as I hear, I judge; and my judgment is just, because I seek not my own will but the will of him who sent me." To his disciples in Samaria at Jacob's Well, when they asked whether or not he had received anything to eat, Jesus said: "My food is to do the will of him who sent me, and to accomplish his work" (Jn 4:34). So just as food is necessary to nourish our life, doing the will of his Father was "food" for Jesus to sustain him in accomplishing the salvation of the world.

Concerning the will of God, Jesus said to his enemies in Jerusalem who marveled at his brilliant teaching because he had not studied under any famous rabbi: "My teaching is not mine, but his who sent me; if any man's will is to do his will, he shall know whether the teaching is from God or whether I am speaking on my own authority. He who speaks on his own authority seeks his own glory, but he who seeks the glory of him who sent him is true, and in him there is no false-hood" (Jn 7:17–18). Jesus seeks only the glory of his Father, so therefore his teaching is true.

In his long discourse on the Eucharist in John 6, Jesus says that the reason for his coming into the world is to do the will of the One who sent him: "For I have come down from heaven, not to do my own will, but the will of him who sent me; and this is the will of him who sent me, that I should lose nothing of all that he has given me, but raise it up at the last day" (vv. 38–40). Here Jesus contrasts his human nature—the human condition that rebels against suffering and death—with the will of his heavenly Father. This truth is expressed even more poignantly when Jesus prays in his Agony in the Garden the night before his Passion: "Father, if thou art willing, remove this cup from me; nevertheless not my will, but thine be done" (Lk 22:42). Jesus freely submits to the will of his heavenly Father that he pour out his blood "for the forgiveness of sins", as the words of Consecration state in the Roman Missal.

The apostle Paul embraced the will of God absolutely in all things. He was dedicated totally to fulfilling that will by spending himself in preaching the gospel and making as many converts as possible. Paul was conscious always of the fact that he was called by God to preach Jesus Christ. This is made clear when he says in the first verse of 1 Corinthians, "Paul, called by the will of God to be an apostle of Christ Jesus", and again in 2 Corinthians 1:1, "Paul, an apostle of

Christ Jesus by the will of God." Saint Paul uses the same expression about the will of God in the opening verse of Ephesians, Colossians, and 2 Timothy.

In his opening greeting in the letter to the Galatians, Saint Paul says that the Lord Jesus Christ "gave himself for our sins to deliver us from the present evil age, according to the will of our God and Father" (1:4).

A beautiful expression about the will of God is found in Saint Paul's first letter to the Thessalonians, when he says to them: "[T]his is the will of God, your sanctification" (4:3). Writing to the whole community, he tells them it is the will of God that they all become saints. That applies to us also—it is the will of God that we become saints. Later on in the same letter Saint Paul says that it is the will of God that we rejoice, pray, and be filled with gratitude to God for his many gifts to us: "Rejoice always, pray constantly, give thanks in all circumstances; for this is the will of God in Christ Jesus for you" (1 Thess 5:16–18).

In the letter to the Hebrews, Paul says clearly that Christ came into this world to do the will of God, which is what Jesus said often during his life and especially during his Agony in the Garden. So Paul says in chapter 10, verses 5–7: "Consequently, when Christ came into the world, he said, 'Sacrifices and offerings you have not desired, but a body have you prepared for me. . . . Then I said, Behold, I have come to do your will, O God, as it is written of me in the roll of the book.'"

Saint Peter in his first letter urges his converts to be obedient to the Roman emperor and all legitimate human authority "for the Lord's sake." And then he goes on to say: "For it is God's will that by doing right you should put to silence the ignorance of foolish men" (1 Pet 2:15). Peter tells them that they should be prepared to defend their faith when others ask them to explain it, but they should do it with "gentleness and reverence" (1 Pet 3:15). They should behave well and be polite in dealing with enemies of the faith, even when they are abused: "For it is better to suffer for doing right, if that should be God's will, than for doing wrong" (1 Pet 3:17). At times it may be God's will that the innocent suffer persecution, as we saw in the case of Job. He repeats the same idea in the next chapter when he says: "Therefore let those who suffer according to God's will do right and entrust their souls to a faithful Creator" (1 Pet 4:19).

Doing the will of God is made equivalent to living forever. Saint John says in his first letter (2:17): "And the world passes away, and the lust of it; but he who does the will of God abides for ever."

God is the Creator of heaven and earth, as we profess in the Nicene Creed at Sunday Mass. Everything that exists, including myself, exists because God willed it. Knowing that he is the source of everything that exists, that I owe my being to him and exist because of him, is a strong motive to learn more about his will from nature and revelation, and to try to the best of my ability to be obedient to him—to do his will. In this regard Saint John says in the book of Revelation that the twenty-four elders fall down before the throne of God in heaven and sing: "Worthy art thou, our Lord and God, to receive glory and honor and power, for you created all things, and by your will they existed and were made" (4:11).

There are many more expressions about the will of God in the New Testament, but these references will give the reader an understanding about how important doing the will of God is in the life of Jesus and his apostles, and how important it is in the life of each person. For, in order to attain the purpose for which we were created by a loving and merciful God, it is essential that we do his will. This is a key phrase in the Our Father: *Thy will be done on earth as it is in heaven.*

7

Divine Grace and the Will of God

Remember your *word* to your servant,
  in which you have made me hope.
This is my comfort in my affliction
  that your *promise* gives me life.
Godless men utterly deride me,
  but I do not turn away from your *law*.
When I think of your *ordinances* from of old,
  I take comfort, O LORD.
Hot indignation seizes me because of the wicked,
  who forsake your *law*.
Your *statutes* have been my songs
  in the house of my pilgrimage.
I remember your name in the night, O LORD,
  and keep your *law*.
This blessing has fallen to me,
  that I have kept your *precepts*.

—Psalm 119:49–56 VII (*Zain*)

God's will embraces both the natural law and the divine revelation that God has destined man for a supernatural end, the face-to-face vision of God in heaven. When we pray "thy will be done" in the Our Father, we are asking God for the grace to abide by his law—both the natural law and the law of the gospel regarding eternal life. The truth is that we cannot do God's will regarding our eternal salvation without the help of his grace—both actual grace and sanctifying grace. We know for sure that God wants everyone to be saved and to attain eternal life. Saint Paul expressed this truth clearly when he wrote, "God . . . desires all men to be saved and to come to the knowledge of the truth" (1 Tim 2:4). In a similar vein he also said, "For this is the will of God, your sanctification" (1 Thess 4:3). Those who are sanctified and die in that state are saints and are destined for heaven.

We know from the Bible and from the teaching of the Church at the Council of Trent and Vatican I that man has a supernatural end, that is, an end that surpasses the requirements of man on the natural level. For personal intimacy with God in heaven is a pure gift that is beyond the requirements of any nature, human or angelic. Acts of any being are proportioned to their end or purpose in life. Thus a dog acts in a way that is in accordance with its nature; a dog cannot think or speak because it is totally immersed in the material world.

Since man has a supernatural end, he must be able to perform supernatural acts that will bring him to that end. This ability or power to perform supernatural acts is what we call "grace", which is a special gift from God above and beyond the requirements of human nature. It affects man's mind and will and enables him to perform supernatural acts. The word itself comes from a Latin word that means "gift". So grace is a special gift from God to enable man to get to heaven.

When we speak about the will of God in this context we are not talking about his will as it exists in his divine essence and is common to all three Persons in the Holy Trinity—an essential aspect of his spirituality and transcendence; we are talking about the *decisions* of his will that affect the created universe and ourselves. In theology this aspect of his will is called his "will of expression" (for example, the Ten Commandments) and his "will of good pleasure" (circumstances that affect me, such as nationality, time, weather, and so forth). So when we pray "thy will be done", it is his will in this regard that we are praying for.

Since God has given man a supernatural end, he needs to act on the level of the supernatural in order to attain that end. Man needs a special help from God to perform such acts; that help is called "grace". The Church teaches that there are two basic kinds of grace: *actual* grace and *sanctifying* grace. Actual grace is a temporary help from God to perform supernatural acts that are meritorious of eternal life. An example of this would be an unbeliever who decides he wants to become a Catholic and to take instructions in the faith. He is assisted in his move toward becoming a Catholic by the help of actual grace.

Sanctifying grace is the supernatural life of the soul that makes us children of God and heirs of heaven. It is a habit of the soul; it is a permanent quality of the soul that makes us participators in the divine nature (see 2 Pet 1:4) and friends of God.

In order to do God's will and attain sanctifying grace, we must first make acts of faith, hope, and charity, and pray and keep the Ten commandments. This is where actual grace comes into the picture. We cannot do God's will without the help of his actual graces, which are often described as enlightenment of the mind and strengthening of the will.

Some actual graces are *external* and others are *internal*. Examples of external graces would be the following: the beautiful liturgy of the Church, the example of the saints and holy people like Blessed Mother Teresa of Calcutta and Saint Padre Pio, reading the Bible, reading a Catholic book, the experience of Catholic charity, and so forth. Internal graces would be an inspiration to pray the Rosary, to practice some self-denial, to make an act of love of God, to desire to become a saint.

Another helpful distinction theologians make regarding grace is that between *efficacious* grace and *sufficient* grace. An efficacious grace is one that is accepted by the human will and acted upon. For example, a man may have an impure temptation; he resists it and prays to our Blessed Mother for help in overcoming it. He gets rid of it, does not sin, and is in peace. That is an efficacious grace. Another person has a similar temptation and makes an attempt to resist, but eventually gives in to the temptation and commits a sin of impurity. We know that with grace no one can be tempted beyond his power to resist. In this latter case, the individual gave in to the temptation and committed the sin. So the grace in this case is called "sufficient", that is, he had the grace to resist but his free will did not accept the help.

The point in each case is that grace enlightens the mind and strengthens the will, but it does not force the will. God made man free and respects his freedom. He deals with each thing according to the nature he gave it. So there is something very mysterious about grace in that it assists the free will but does not force it to do the right thing.

Since God wills our sanctification and salvation, and both are supernatural, he obliges himself to give us the grace we need in order to carry out his will. God is all-powerful and present to every reality, living or non-living. He is present to every atom in my body and to every moment of my existence. God does not expect the impossible from anyone or anything. If he did, it would be unjust, but that cannot be since God is infinite justice and mercy.

Natural things, such as minerals, plants, and animals, as we have mentioned before, do what they do, accomplish their purpose in the universe, by necessity. There is no freedom in subhuman material realities. This means that divine grace concerns human beings and human freedom. Of all the things on earth, man is the only one that chooses his own end. That is because he has an intellect and a free will. Through the revelation of Jesus Christ and the teaching of the

Catholic Church, we know with certainty that the goal or end of human existence is not to be found in this temporal life on earth. Since the soul is immortal, it will live forever. God has told us that our final end, after death, is to be with him in heaven forever in complete happiness—a happiness so great that we cannot even imagine it, as Saint Paul says in one of his letters.

We will attain heaven by doing the will of God, by conforming our wills to his will. He always gives us the grace we need in order to keep the commandments and to avoid mortal sin, the death of the soul. That is his will of expression. His will of good pleasure has to do with things that are beyond the control of our will, like health and sickness, good weather and bad weather, long life or short life, honor or dishonor, success or failure, and so forth. In these matters the lowest level of doing God's will is resignation or acceptance of what happens to me. The highest level of conformity is to embrace all of these things explicitly as the will of God, whether in health or sickness, life or death. Saint Ignatius of Loyola, the founder of the Jesuits, said that the goal of the Christian life is to find God in all things, since they are all a manifestation of his will. We will treat this matter more in detail in the next chapter on divine providence.

8

Providence and the Will of God

The LORD is my portion;
    I promise to keep your *words.*
I entreat your favor with all my heart;
    be gracious to me according to your *promise.*
When I think of your ways,
    I turn my feet to your *testimonies.*
I hasten and do not delay
    to keep your *commandments.*
Though the cords of the wicked ensnare me,
    I do not forget your *law.*
At midnight I rise to praise you,
    because of your righteous *ordinances.*
I am a companion of all who fear you,
    of those who keep your *precepts.*
The earth, O LORD, is full of your steadfast love;
    teach me your *statutes*!

—Psalm 119:57–64 VIII (*Heth*)

Saint John tells us that God is love (1 Jn 4:16). Love is an act of the will of God that follows upon his knowledge. God is infinite in being and perfection; he is also infinite in knowledge, will, and power. He is the Creator of heaven and earth, of all things visible and invisible, as we pray in the Creed at Mass. God created out of nothing everything in the universe—immense bodies like the trillions of stars, and very small things like atoms, electrons, and ions. God is therefore the source of all existence—not only to bring things into existence, but also to keep them in existence. If he were to forget or ignore some thing, it would cease to exist and fall into the nothingness from which it came. This means then that God is present to everything that exists and that he knows each thing. Jesus touched on this point when he told the multitude "even the hairs of your head are numbered" (Lk 12:7).

Since with God there is no time—he transcends time—all time of past, present, and future is part of his knowledge. He sees it all at once. For God there is no past or future—everything that ever was or will be is present to him, similar to the way I am aware of the present moment. This is what we mean by God's providence, which is his foresight or foreknowledge.

God had a plan or purpose in creating the universe, including the angels. Because he is infinite goodness, and love means *wishing good to others, the purpose or goal of creation is to communicate his goodness to others. The final goal of all things is the* goodness of God himself, since he cannot have any purpose outside of himself. Thus the all-wise plan for the universe in the mind of God, and the execution of this plan by his will, is called "providence".[1] So God's providence means that he knows everything in this world and directs all things to the end or purpose for which they were created. Thus when we reflect on the will of God as it affects the world, and us, we are reflecting on divine providence, since providence includes both the plan in the mind of God and the will to produce it. The latter, which occurs in time, is called God's governance of the world.

God's providence extends to all natural things and also to man. The former is called *natural* providence and the latter is called *supernatural* providence. In the area of nature—elements, plants, and animals—God's will is carried out necessarily. These things act according to their nature, but God deals with man differently than he does with nature. There are two reasons for this.

The first reason is that man has an intellect and a free will. That is because he is made in the image and likeness of God (Gen 1:26). All things below man have their end or purpose set for them by God, who made them. So bees, for example, fly and make honey because that is their nature given to them by God, who created them. Man, however, because he possesses free will, chooses his end. He has reason and natural law to guide him in his choices, but he can decide to act unreasonably and against his nature, which subhuman beings cannot do.

---

[1] See John A. Hardon, S.J., *Modern Catholic Dictionary* (New York: Doubleday, 1980), p. 448.

The second reason is that God has given man a supernatural end, that is, the face-to-face vision of God in heaven after his temporal, earthly life. Man's nature as such does not require this; it is an added gift above and beyond the gift of nature. That is God's will for man. So, in order to attain his end, man must freely embrace God's will for him. God has revealed this will in a beginning, imperfect way in the Old Testament, and completely by Jesus Christ, who is both God and man. So now, in order to attain his end, a man must have faith in Jesus Christ and live according to his commandment to love God and neighbor, since that is a summary of the will of God as expressed in the New Testament revelation, in tradition, and in the teaching of the Church.

Man cannot attain his supernatural end by his efforts alone, because his final end—union with God—is beyond his natural powers. So he needs a special help from God in order to achieve it. That help is found in God's grace, imparted to us through the infinite merits of Jesus Christ, which he gained for us by his life, death, and Resurrection.

God has not revealed to us how many human beings will be saved, but we may hope that it is the majority. It seems to me more probable that his grace will be successful for most of us rather than a failure. It is not likely, considering the universal salvific will of God (1 Tim 2:4), that Satan, a creature, will defeat the grace of God regarding the salvation of most human persons. But this matter remains hidden from us, so it is a deep mystery.

A serious problem concerning providence and the will of God is the existence of evil in the world—both physical evil and moral evil. Evil is not something positive, as the Manicheans and their followers have thought. Evil is the lack or absence of some good that ought to be present in something that already exists. Thus, blindness and cancer are physical evils; sin, which is a violation or rejection of God's will, is a moral evil, a disruption of the order that should exist between a man and his Creator. But plants and animals cannot sin because they do not have free will and so follow their nature by necessity.

What is the problem? The problem is that God is infinitely good and everything he does is good and is in accordance with his infinite goodness. If that is so, and it is, and if God created everything, why is there evil in the world? If God is all-knowing, all-good, and all-powerful, then why is there suffering and sin in the world? The greatest human minds have grappled with this perennial problem and have tried to give a satisfactory answer.

The best general answer was given by Saint Augustine, who said that God is so powerful that he can bring good out of evil. For example, a man in mortal sin, and so an enemy of God, comes down suddenly with terminal cancer and has only a few months to live. Realizing his sinful state and his mortality, he repents of his sins, makes a good confession, receives Holy Communion and the Anointing of the Sick, and so prepares himself to die in the state of sanctifying grace.

He dies and goes to heaven, so attaining the end for which he was created. He obtains that end because of his free choice, aided by divine grace.

Some theologians have wondered whether or not God's providence extends to every particular thing or to just the world in general. Saint Thomas Aquinas says that it extends to everything that exists, large and small, past, present, and future. The reason is that all things are foreseen by God and kept in existence by him, as we have seen. This includes both necessary and contingent causes. Providence, therefore, is universal, immediate, certain, and gentle or without violence—that is, God governs all things in accordance with their nature. So he accomplishes his purpose through natural laws.

If God has foreknowledge of everything, then how does one explain the existence of chance or fortuitous events? Chance happens because particular causes cross each other contrary to their intention, as in the case of an automobile accident. To the individual it is an accident, but to God, who is the universal cause of everything, it is foreseen and permitted for reasons that are hidden from us. This is especially the case in fatal accidents when someone accidentally walks in front of a moving truck and is killed.

We have used the words "necessary" and "contingent". Something is necessary if it must be or must exist. Something is contingent if it cannot be; it is possible for it not to exist. The point here is that, just because God's providence is universal and he knows everything that will happen, it does not follow that everything happens by necessity. As we have said, dogs produce dogs, not cats, and oak trees produce oak trees, not apple trees. They do not have free choice but are determined by their nature to some definite thing. It is necessary for every effect to have a cause, and composed things can cease to exist, so they are called "contingent". God, the universal Creator, produced some causes that are necessary and some that are contingent.

The situation with man is different. Man has a free will. He can follow God's will for him and become a saint. He can also reject God's will and become a sinner and an enemy of God. Just because God knows what each person he creates will do with his free will, it does not follow that man acts out of necessity. Of course, it remains quite mysterious to us that God can create free persons, whom he keeps in existence, who can oppose him and say, "I will not serve!" Those who are saved and attain their final end in heaven glorify his goodness and mercy. Those who are lost and go to hell glorify God's justice. God does not predestine anyone to hell, but by his permissive will he allows individual persons to misuse their freedom by rebelling against him.

Many things happen to us that are not under the control of our will. I refer here to such things as the family we are born into, our parents and relatives, sex, time of birth, nationality, personal talents, and many other things. All of these things fall under God's providence and his will for us. Theologians refer to these things as the result of God's "will of good pleasure". It also includes such things as night and day, sun and rain, and many of the small things that happen to us each day.

It is God's will that we become holy persons. That means he wants us to become perfect. In the Sermon on the Mount Jesus says to each one of us, "You, therefore, must be perfect, as your heavenly Father is perfect" (Mt 5:48). The key and the way to perfection is conformity of our will with the will of God—both his will of expression as given in his commandments and counsels, and also in his will of good pleasure. The person who tries to conform his will to God's will is pleasing to God and is on his way to heaven and eternal salvation.

Theologians such as Saint Thomas Aquinas prove from divine revelation that God is immutable because he is the fullness of all being, or infinite being. He already possesses everything, so he cannot gain anything. God is all act and has no potency; therefore he cannot change. He has willed this world into existence and he knows with absolute certitude who will be saved and who will be lost. That being the case, then why should anyone pray and ask God for some good thing, or ask to be freed from some illness? Saint Paul tells us in one of his letters that he asked the Lord three times to be freed from some affliction, but the Lord refused and said that his grace was sufficient for him. This was to keep Paul humble.

The answer to the question about why we should pray is to be found in the universality of God's knowledge and power. First of all, we find many examples of prayer in the Bible. The patriarchs prayed and the prophets prayed. God answered some of their prayers, and some of them he did not answer. In the New Testament, Jesus is a model of prayer. He prayed before selecting his twelve apostles, and he prayed in the Garden of Gethsemane before his Passion and death. When his disciples asked him to teach them how to pray he gave them the Our Father (Mt 6:9–13). The Lord Jesus says in Luke 18:1 that we "ought always to pray and not lose heart". Saint Paul tells us in 1 Thessalonians 5:17 to "pray constantly".

Saint Thomas Aquinas says in one of his articles on prayer that God wants us to pray and ask him for what we need. He says further that God will not give us certain things unless we ask for them.[2] In this context, if you do not pray and ask for what you want, you will not receive it. Our Lord himself says on this point: "Ask, and it will be given you; seek, and you will find; knock, and it will be opened to you" (Mt 7:7).

Many prayers are not answered the way we want them to be answered. God is infinite goodness, and everything he does is good. Many people pray for things that might not be good for them, such as winning twenty million dollars in a lottery. God does not grant these requests because they would not help the person to save his soul. Often prayers are answered in a way we do not understand, but in the long run the answer is for our own good or for the good of others,

[2] *STh* II–II, 83, 2.

such as asking for a cure from cancer. The cure is not granted, but the person dies in the state of grace with the sacraments of the Church and so attains his eternal salvation.

The providence of God involves both his knowledge and his will. The way for man to attain human perfection, and eventually eternal life, is to conform his will to the will of God. The more perfect that conformity is, the more one becomes like God and so is on the way to eternal life. These reflections should help each person to pray humbly and sincerely each day, "Thy will be done on earth as it is in heaven".

9

Sin and the Will of God

You have dealt well with your servant,
    O Lord, according to your *word*.
Teach me good judgment and knowledge,
    for I believe in your *commandments*.
Before I was afflicted I went astray,
    but now I keep your *word*.
You are good and do good;
    teach me your *statutes*.
The godless besmear me with lies,
    but with my whole heart I keep your *precepts*;
their heart is gross like fat,
    but I delight in your *law*.
It is good for me that I was afflicted,
    that I might learn your *statutes*.
The *law* of your mouth is better to me
    than thousands of gold and silver pieces.

—Psalm 119:65–72 IX (*Teth*)

Jesus urges us to pray to our heavenly Father, "Thy will be done on earth as it is in heaven." To do the will of God means to obey him in everything that concerns him. To go against his will, to rebel against him and to follow one's own will, is called a *sin*. The

Catechism of the Catholic Church, quoting Saint Augustine and Saint Thomas Aquinas, defines a sin as "an utterance, a deed, or a desire contrary to the eternal law".[1] The eternal law, the natural law, and the revealed law in the Bible are various manifestations of the will of God. Therefore, a violation of any of those laws as a thought, word, or deed contrary to the will of God is a sin. Thus it is clear that there is an essential connection between sin and the will of God.

A sin is a voluntary act proceeding from a spiritual person endowed with intellect and will. Only angels and men are spiritual persons, so only angels and men can sin. All other creatures, living and non-living, have a nature given to them by God, their Creator, and so their purpose or end has been assigned to them. They are not free to choose their end, as men and angels can do. This means that they cannot commit a sin. Cows and horses act according to their nature and are not capable of sin. Plants, animals, weather, sun, moon, and stars cannot sin because they are not personal beings.

Everything a man has—soul and body, with their various powers—is a gift from God. Man is a thinking, reasonable being. He does not act from instinct, as birds do. His guide is his reason; God gave him an intellect to be his guide in life. His reason tells him to do good and to avoid evil in his relations with God, with his neighbor, and with himself.

---

[1] *Catechism of the Catholic Church* (St. Pauls/Libreria Editrice Vaticana, 1994), no. 1849. Hereafter abbreviated *CCC*.

Because of the sin of Adam and Eve, man lost the grace of God and the preternatural gifts of integrity and immortality. As a result man suffers from concupiscence, that is, a tendency toward pride and disobedience that often leads him to sin or rebel against God and his law.

Because God has revealed it to us, as Christians we know that the reason for our existence on this earth is to get to heaven. The length of man's life is three score and ten years. According to Psalm 90, those who are strong live about eighty years, and then they die. We also know from reason and revelation that man's soul is immortal, so death is not the end of all life; death for the saved means a change of life. What once was a body on earth in time and space is now a living, immortal spirit in the presence of God until the end of the world, when man's glorified soul will be reunited with his body.

Jesus Christ has revealed to us that our life in the next world is supernatural. That means that God has given us a purpose in life that is above and beyond the demands of our human nature. He has destined us for a personal union with him in perfect happiness for all eternity.

How does a human person attain the end for which he was created? He attains it by doing God's will in this life. He attains it by avoiding all mortal sin, which is the death of the soul. He attains it by living a life of virtue by obeying God's commandments. Jesus sums up the whole law and the prophets: You shall love the

Lord your God with all your heart, and with all your soul, and with all your mind, . . . and love your neighbor as yourself" (Mt 22:37, 39). The person who does that is a friend of God and lives in the state of sanctifying grace. That person has achieved the purpose for which he was created. When he dies he will go to heaven either immediately or after having been purified by the temporal punishment due to him in purgatory.

The saints that we honor in the Church are noble individuals who have controlled their unruly passions, practiced virtue and asceticism, and lived a life of love of God and neighbor. They have attained the end or purpose for which they were created. As such, they are models for us, and the Church urges us to imitate them. The supreme model of virtue, of course, is our Lord and Savior, Jesus Christ. We save our souls by following him and imitating him. After him we have the example of our Blessed Mother, Mary, and Saint Joseph, her spouse and foster father of Jesus during his early life in Egypt and Nazareth.

Sin is any word, deed, or desire contrary to the law and will of God. Since sin flows from the will of man, it is voluntary. Will is the source of morality. So good deeds are called moral, and evil or sinful deeds are called immoral. A serious or mortal sin has three components: (1) serious matter, like blasphemy; (2) sufficient reflection—one must know that the thought, word, or deed is forbidden by God; (3) full consent of the will. If any of these is lacking or deficient, then the deed is either a venial sin or no sin at all. Thus, infants and children before the age of reason cannot sin; a person cannot sin while sleeping or dreaming because he cannot think clearly and give full consent of the will.

If we reflect on the relationship between God and man, we must come to realize that everything we have and are is a pure gift from God. He is our greatest benefactor. He has made man free and the master of his own fate. God is so powerful that he can create a creature like man, who can refuse to obey him; man can reject God and choose some earthly thing as his last end. For some it is money; for others it is sex; for others it is power; for others it is food and drink.

Since man is wholly indebted to God for everything he is, it follows that the greatest evil in the world is mortal sin, which is a grave offense against his Creator and Benefactor. God is infinitely good, infinitely loving and lovable. Love is his nature (1 Jn 4:16); he created man because of his love for him and seeks a return of love. The mortal sinner turns his back on God and worships some creature in his place. This is an act of the greatest ingratitude. Therefore, it is no exaggeration to say that mortal sin is the greatest evil in the world. The consequences of unrepented sin are eternal, since the mortal sinner, if he dies in that state, will go immediately to hell and be there not just for a period of years, but for all eternity. Is it possible to imagine a fate worse than that?

Outside of sin, all the evils in this world—disease, cancer, heart attack, stroke, and sufferings of all kinds—are temporary. They will come to an end, and if they are accepted with faith and love as being in accordance with the permissive will of God, they merit an increase of grace and glory for eternal life. Mortal sin as the rejection of the will of God has unhappy eternal consequences. A contemporary author said some years ago that ideas have consequences. As followers of Jesus Christ, who is both God and man, we know with infallible certainty that mortal sin has unhappy eternal consequences. Those who die in that state will spend eternity separated from God, hating God and grinding their teeth in the outer darkness.

Let us now resolve to do the will of God always and to avoid the misery and slavery of mortal sin. God is infinite goodness, and everything he wills is good. Therefore our personal fulfillment and happiness are found only in uniting our will with the holy will of God.

10

Doing the Will of God

Your hands have made and fashioned me;
  give me understanding that I may learn your
  commandments.
Those who fear you shall see me and rejoice,
  because I have hoped in your *word.*
I know, O LORD, that your *judgments* are right,
  and that in faithfulness you have afflicted me.
Let your mercy be ready to comfort me
  according to your *promise* to your servant.
Let your compassion come to me, that I may live;
  for your *law* is my delight.
Let the godless be put to shame,
  because they have subverted me with guile;
  as for me, I will meditate on your *precepts.*
Let those who fear you turn to me,
  that they may know your *testimonies.*
May my heart be blameless in your *statutes,*
  that I may not be put to shame!

—Psalm 119:73–80 X (*Yod*)

It is one thing to know the will of God with the mind,
but it is something else, something different, to actually do the will of God, obey his commandments, and

conform our will to his will in all the events and circumstances of our lives. Saints and holy persons,
whether priests, nuns, or laypeople, unite their will
with the will of God and seek to show their love for
him in everything they think, do, or desire. That is a
high level of spirituality and is a sign of the perfection
that the Lord Jesus tells us we should strive for (see
Mt 5:48). Given our sinful nature, given our passions,
and given the concupiscence we have inherited from
Adam and Eve, that is not easy to accomplish. Some
achieve it early in life. There are many examples: Saint
Bernadette, the Fatima children, Saint Aloysius Gon-
zaga, Saint Stanislaus Kostka, Saint Maria Goretti, Saint
Dominic Savio, and many others.

Other, older saints, some with strong passions and
sinful pasts, had to struggle to reach a high level of Christian perfection, but once they started some of them
reached great perfection rather quickly. In this regard,
Saint Augustine, Saint Francis of Assisi, Saint Ignatius
Loyola, Saint Teresa of Avila, Saint Charles de Fou-
cauld, and the Venerable Matt Talbot come to mind.

Union with God for all eternity is the end or purpose of human existence. As we learned in catechism
class, the answer to the question: Why did God make
me? is to know, love, and serve him in this life, and to
be happy with him forever in the next. We love him
and serve him by doing his will. Where do we find
that will? We find that will in the Ten Commandments, in the counsels of the Lord, and also in the
Beatitudes.

God desires the salvation of all and that all come to knowledge of the truth about God, man, and the world (1 Tim 2:4). We also find the will of God in the ordinary circumstances of daily life—family, work, study, recreation, and friendship.

As Catholics we are blessed by being active members of the one, holy, catholic, and apostolic Church founded by Jesus Christ on Saint Peter and the other apostles. The Church points the way to heaven for us and assists us in living a godly life by the grace we receive from the sacraments, from the preaching of the gospel, and from personal prayer.

There are various levels of salvation. Some men and women just barely get to heaven by avoiding mortal sins, but do no more and do not strive to be saints; others strive for Christian perfection by trying to do God's will in every aspect of life. God wants us not only to be saved but also to become perfect—to attain Christian perfection. That is clear from Matthew 5:48 and 1 Thessalonians 4:3, which have already been quoted in previous chapters (see p. 61 and pp. 11, 49 respectively). Perfection consists in complete fulfillment of the law of God, for the law is the manifestation of the will of God.

It is not easy to obey God's law completely all the time. The reason for this is that man has a fallen human nature. Not only does he come into this world without the grace of God and so needs baptism to regain it, but he is also burdened with concupiscence, a tendency toward sin and rebellion against God that manifests itself especially in sins of pride and sensuality. Saint John summed up concupiscence by referring to the "lust" of the flesh and the "pride of life" (1 Jn 2:16).

God's grace, however, is always there to help us overcome temptation, since no one is tempted beyond his ability to resist. Still, there are many obstacles to overcome in order to avoid all deliberate sin; spiritual growth requires daily prayer, frequent Communion and confession, and the practice of some self-denial. One spiritual author says that Christian perfection is achieved by love and sacrifice.[1]

There are both interior and exterior obstacles to growth in holiness and conformity to the will of God. Interior obstacles exist in both the soul and the body. In his soul man is exposed to the danger of pride and vanity—the temptation to put oneself in the place of God. In man's body there is the problem with the passions, often referred to as the *irascible* and the *concupiscible* appetites. The first has to do with anger, and the latter with sensuality in the form of sexual desires and excess in the matter of food and drink. Giving in to sensuality results in sins like fornication, adultery, masturbation, gluttony, and drunkenness.

There are also exterior obstacles to growth in holiness. They are the world and the devil. Our Lord warns us again and again in the Gospels not to love the world because of its vanity and opposition to God. We see

---

[1] Adolphe Tanquerey, S.S. *The Spiritual Life* (Rockford, Ill.: Tan Books, 2000), p. 175.

this every day in our society. The message of the major media—print, radio, and television—is almost completely one of self-gratification: Enjoy yourself. Sex is entertainment. Money produces happiness. Do whatever you feel like doing, and you will be happy. It was summarized long ago in the epigram: "Eat, drink and be merry, for tomorrow you will die." This is a message of despair that leads, eventually, to bitterness, unhappiness, and death.

Another external obstacle to growth in union with God is the devil. There is something very mysterious about the devil. He is a created spiritual being, a fallen angel whom God allows to tempt and harass us. We have good examples of this in the temptation of Eve in Paradise (Gen 3), in the book of Job in the Old Testament, and in the temptation of Jesus in the wilderness (Mt 4:1–11). The devil is no laughing matter. Saint Peter says that he goes about the world like a roaring lion seeking whom he may destroy (1 Pet 5:8). We are all subject to temptations from the devil, who seeks to seduce us into mortal sin, and therefore we should avoid all voluntary contact with him. This includes having nothing to do with Ouija boards, séances, tarot cards, and so forth. While his power is very limited and can always be overcome with the grace of Jesus Christ, the devil is a tyrant over those who submit to his control; he is very clever, as is obvious from his temptation of Eve in the Garden of Eden. God allows the devil to tempt us for his own reasons, so that by resisting him we can demonstrate our love for God. In a sense, temptation is a test of fidelity. Job was frightfully tormented by Satan, but he never lost his faith and trust in God, accepting his suffering as the will of God. To his wife, who urged him to curse God and die, Job said: "You speak as one of the foolish women would speak. Shall we receive good at the hand of God, and shall we not receive evil? In all this Job did not sin with his lips" (Job 2:10).

As I said above, it is one thing to know the will of God, and it is another thing to actually embrace it and do it. Given man's fallen nature and tendency toward pride and self-assertion, in order to do God's will man needs the help of God's grace. Grace is a supernatural help from God to do good and to avoid evil. Grace enlightens the mind and strengthens the will. God in his mercy offers his help to every individual because he desires all to be saved, even though they have a free will and can reject him. Actual graces are temporal helps to overcome temptation, or they are given by God as inspirations to do some good act; sanctifying grace is a permanent quality of the soul that elevates man to the supernatural level and makes him a new creature in the spiritual order—a child of God and an heir of heaven. Since God has destined man for a supernatural end, to be united with him in knowledge and love in heaven forever, he has bound himself to give man the graces he needs in order to attain his end.

God is the efficient cause of grace; Jesus is the meritorious cause of grace, who merited infinite grace for us by his life, Passion, and death on the Cross on Calvary. That grace is communicated to us in many different ways, mainly through the Church. The normal channels of grace are the sacraments, especially baptism, the Holy Eucharist, and penance. These instruments of grace remain ineffective if we do not make use of them.

Essential for growth in holiness and doing God's will in all things is regular prayer, both vocal and mental. No one can be saved without some prayer, even if it is just a short ejaculation like "Jesus, have mercy on me!"

Spiritual authors for centuries have taught that there are three levels of holiness or perfection. They are the purgative way, the illuminative way, and the unitive way. Very briefly, the first stage, the purgative way, means that the individual avoids all mortal sin and strives to remain in the state of grace all the time. The second stage, the illuminative way, means that the individual avoids all deliberate venial sins. The third and highest stage, the unitive way, means that the individual not only avoids all venial sins but also strives to rid himself of all semi-deliberate venial sins and all imperfections and faults of character. In short, such a person strives 24/7 to do God's will in all things both great and small.

To achieve this level of Christian perfection it is necessary to follow a plan or a rule of life. That rule is spelled out for monks and nuns in their constitutions. The Church has also given definite guidelines for priests to follow in order to grow in perfection. In addition to daily Mass and praying the Liturgy of the Hours (Divine Office), priests are urged to practice some daily mental prayer, recite the Rosary, do some spiritual reading, and make visits to the Blessed Sacrament. Archbishop Fulton J. Sheen in his retreats for priests always urged them to make a daily Holy Hour before the Blessed Sacrament, as he did for over fifty years.

Laypeople also need a plan to grow in holiness. On a basic level, this includes Sunday Mass and Communion, regular confession, a daily Rosary, reading the Bible, and saying some vocal prayers. It also includes some good works, like helping others and donating to charitable causes when they can. Short prayers during the day also help, such as saying occasionally, "Jesus, Mary, and Joseph", or "Most Sacred Heart of Jesus, I implore that I may ever love thee more and more", or the Divine Mercy prayer, "Jesus, I trust in you." These and similar prayers are a great help to remind oneself of the constant presence of God and to help one fulfill the regular duties of daily life.

If we are going to imitate Christ and follow him, it is necessary to practice some self-denial or asceticism. This is not a popular topic these days, since our culture preaches constantly that one should practice self-indulgence—get the most out of life, forget about death, and don't think about God and eternity. But to truly love God it is necessary to practice some self-denial. This means that we must control our passions and reject all the temptations that come our way. This is not easy to do. To help us achieve self-control the Church recommends a certain amount of fasting, prayer, and almsgiving; that is one of the reasons for the forty days of Lent. There is nothing like fasting to remind us that we are mere creatures and that we are totally dependent on God. Fasting brings some humility into our Christian life. If we follow Christ we must carry our Cross as he did. As Jesus said to his disciples, "If any man would come after me, let him deny himself and take up his cross and follow me" (Mt 16:24). Love of God is the essence of perfection, but love requires sacrifice; it is not all joy and sweetness. That is true with regard to love between human beings, and it is also true with regard to love of God.

A great help in striving to do the will of God is the example of Jesus, his Blessed Mother, and the great saints of the Church like the apostles, Saint Paul, Saint Francis of Assisi, Saint Thérèse of Lisieux, and many others. We get to know Jesus by prayer, by assisting at the liturgy of the Church, and by reading the Gospels; we get to know the saints by reading good books on the lives of the saints. We all like a good story—that is why films are popular. The best of all stories are the life of Jesus and the lives of his saints. They show us the way. The saints are proof that weak human beings can, with the help of God, attain a high level of Christian perfection, which is nothing other than love of God and embracing his will in all things. Those who do the will of God in all things can truly say with Saint Paul, "I have been crucified with Christ; it is no longer I who live, but Christ who lives in me" (Gal 2:20).

In order to grow in the love of God and conformity to the will of God it is necessary to practice some asceticism. Today this idea is not often mentioned, and it is even less often recommended. To love God means to will his good and glory, and we do that by doing his will. By doing that, we glorify God and we also work out our own salvation. For these reasons Jesus teaches us to pray in the Our Father, "Thy will be done on earth as it is in heaven."

II

Suffering and the Will of God

My soul languishes for your salvation;
   I hope in your *word*.
My eyes fail with watching for your *promise*;
   I ask, "When will you comfort me?"
For I have become like a wineskin in the smoke,
   yet I have not forgotten your *statutes*.
How long must your servant endure?
   When will you *judge* those who persecute me?
Godless men have dug pitfalls for me,
   men who do not conform to your *law*.
All your *commandments* are sure;
   they persecute me with falsehood; help me!
They have almost made an end of me on earth;
   but I have not forsaken your *precepts*.
In your mercy spare my life,
   that I may keep the *testimonies* of your mouth.

—Psalm 119:81–88 XI (*Caph*)

No human being can live without suffering. Our mother suffers in giving us birth, and the first sound we make is a cry of pain asking for food, warmth, and affection. Every day of our life we suffer something—hunger, thirst, disappointment, mental stress, weariness, and other physical needs. We acknowledge daily suffering every time we pray the Morning Offering: "O Jesus, through the Immaculate Heart of Mary, I offer you all of my prayers, works, joys and *sufferings* of this day." We all have to die. Some die slowly and others die swiftly, but we all suffer in order to leave this world of time and space and enter into eternity. Our culture tends to hide and ignore the universality of suffering. A common trick of politicians is to blame it on someone else. The need to suffer, however, is intrinsic to our human nature, which is a composition of body and spirit.

Suffering is closely related to pain, either physical or moral. Father John A. Hardon, S.J., defines suffering as "the disagreeable experience of soul that comes with the presence of evil or the privation of some good." [1] In giving the reason for suffering, Father Hardon goes on to say that

> in the present order of Providence suffering is the result of sin having entered the world. Its purpose, however, is not only to expiate wrongdoing, but to enable the believer to offer God a sacrifice of praise of his divine right over creatures, to unite oneself with Christ in his sufferings as an expression of love, and in the process to become more like Christ, who, having joy set before him, chose the Cross, and thus "to complete what is lacking in Christ's afflictions for the sake of his body, that is, the church (Col. 1:24)." [2]

[1] Hardon, *Modern Catholic Dictionary*, p. 521.
[2] Ibid., p. 523.

There is an essential connection between suffering and sin. In Genesis 3 it is stated very clearly that, as a result of their sin, Adam and Eve were expelled from Paradise and made subject to suffering and, eventually, death. The first death occurred when Cain murdered his brother Abel.

There is something very mysterious about suffering. Most—perhaps all—human beings feel, almost instinctively, that there is something wrong in the world, that suffering and death somehow should not exist. This feeling becomes most acute when one reflects on the nature of God and comes to see that he is infinite goodness and infinite love, and that everything he does is good. How then explain the presence of so much suffering and evil in the world? From Genesis in the Old Testament to Revelation in the New Testament, the Bible's clear answer to this pressing question is that suffering is the punishment for man's sin, for the misuse of his freedom in rebelling against God. God made Adam and Eve immortal and free from suffering. Their subsequent suffering, and ours, is the result of their sin against a good and loving God. They were warned, but they did not heed the warning—they were tricked by the deceit of the devil, Satan. As punishment for their sin they suffered pain and death, and transmitted this to all of their descendents. Their punishment was just because of their pride and disobedience to the loving God who created them from nothing.

Since suffering is a part of divine providence, it is something willed by God. Theologians refer to this as his "permissive" will, that is, he permits suffering to happen because of the misuse of free will on the part of our first parents and also because of our own personal sins.

The primary model of suffering and how to deal with it is, of course, our divine Savior, Jesus Christ. He was born in poverty; Herod sought to kill him so he had to flee into Egypt; in Nazareth he led a life of poverty and hard work for almost thirty years. During his public life the Scribes and Pharisees persecuted him; Judas, one of his apostles, betrayed him; and finally, he suffered a very painful, humiliating death on the Cross on Calvary. Jesus was the suffering servant described in Isaiah 52–53; he was the suffering Messiah, especially as presented in Saint Mark's Gospel, where Jesus predicts three times that he would suffer and die in Jerusalem (Mk 8:31; 9:31; 10:33). In the Nicene Creed that we pray at Mass we say, "For our sake he was crucified under Pontius Pilate, he suffered death and was buried". His Mother also suffered along with Jesus. We commemorate her suffering in the devotion to the Seven Sorrows of the Blessed Virgin Mary.

Jesus not only accepted his sufferings, but he also embraced them because they were the will of his Father. To his disciples who asked him to eat, Jesus said, "My food is to do the will of him who sent me, and to accomplish his work" (Jn 4:34). On another occasion he said, "I seek not my own will but the will of him who sent me" (Jn 5:30). This attitude of Jesus to the will of his

Father is repeated in the midst of his Agony in the Garden of Gethsemane when he said, "Father . . . not my will, but yours, be done" (Lk 22:42).

We must not forget that Jesus is a suffering Savior, a suffering Redeemer, a suffering Messiah. We come into this world to live; Jesus came into this world to die. Jesus was totally obedient to his heavenly Father in all things, and thus he merited infinite grace for us, and for himself a name that is above every other name, as Saint Paul says so eloquently in Phillippians 2:11. If we love him and obey him and so do his will, he and his Father and the Holy Spirit will come to us and be with us, as Jesus said to his disciples: "If a man loves me, he will keep my word, and my Father will love him, and we will come to him and make our home with him" (Jn 14:23). But it was God's will that Jesus should suffer in order to save us and to enter into his glory, as Jesus said to his apostles after his Resurrection: "Was it not necessary that the Christ should suffer these things and enter into his glory?" (Lk 24:26).

Jesus is the Savior of the whole human race. Our redemption was accomplished at a great price—the suffering and death of Jesus Christ, both God and man. Suffering was necessary as atonement for the offense of sins against God, the Creator of the whole universe. No mere creature could make adequate satisfaction to God for the sins of mankind; only the God-man, Jesus, whose deeds have an infinite value, could make adequate satisfaction for the evil of sin.

And that is what Jesus did by the Passion and death that he suffered for us, not for himself, since he was absolutely sinless. He suffered for us and saved us because of his love for us. We were made for God, and Jesus brings it about that we can finally attain the face-to-face vision of God in heaven if we die in the state of sanctifying grace.

Human suffering, if accepted in the right spirit of union with Jesus and in obedience to our heavenly Father, has salvific value.[3] That means that it helps us gain the grace of God. Suffering with Christ has a purifying effect that helps us to realize that we are mere creatures and are totally dependent on God. Suffering is a good teacher—it teaches us humility; it teaches us to realize that God is everything and we are nothing. Suffering also merits satisfaction for personal sins and for the sins of others.

Jesus had compassion for those who suffered from various diseases. During his public life he cured hundreds of sick people, and raised three of them from the dead. The resurrected Christ identifies himself with those who suffer hunger, thirst, sickness, and nakedness, as is clear from his words at the Last Judgment in Matthew 25:31–46.

It is a shame that so much human suffering is wasted because it is not accepted in the right spirit. Only the

[3] Pope John Paul II wrote an excellent apostolic exhortation in 1984 on the salvific value of suffering: "On the Christian Meaning of Human Suffering" (*Salvifici Doloris*).

faithful, prayerful Christian knows how to benefit from suffering because he knows that it is the will of God and he submits to that. He prays to be delivered from his suffering, but it is always within the context of the will of God; he does not despair but always has hope. Hospitals are huge buildings that contain a tremendous amount of human suffering. People go there because they are sick and suffering and they hope to find relief and a cure. But hospitals are places where men and women of all ages suffer and die. Catholic hospitals were established to come to the aid of the sick, to see Christ in each sick person, as Blessed Teresa of Calcutta did, and to help them get to heaven. Modern medicine is able to alleviate much physical pain and suffering, but there is pain in the recovery from surgery and the mental anguish connected with going to a hospital for surgery or other treatment.

Human beings cannot get through life without suffering, no matter how rich or talented they may be. Suffering is an evil—it is the absence of some good. God allows this for his own good reasons, which are hidden from us. Sin and suffering relate to the existence of free will on the part of angels and men; they result from the misuse of that freedom. God has shown us the way to happiness by keeping his law, but we are free to follow it or to reject it. That is why there is something very mysterious about suffering. God is so all-powerful that he can create beings who are free to say no to him and to suffer the consequences. Since God permits suffering, and because it is redemptive and unavoidable, for a Christian there are various ways of dealing with it.

The first level is acceptance of what God sends our way, and especially acceptance of the duties of one's state in life. This is necessary in order to avoid serious sin and to remain in the state of grace. The second level is resignation in accepting the crosses that God sends our way—weariness, sickness, loss of a loved one, blindness, terminal cancer, and so forth. The third and higher level is the voluntary embrace of self-denial and mortification—fasting, almsgiving, no smoking or drinking, no sweets, volunteer work, and so forth. The value of mortification is that it not only makes reparation for sins committed, but it also strengthens the will to resist temptations. Those who practice self-denial are the ones who are truly free—they are free because they are in control of their passions and emotions. Reason dominates in their life, not feelings.

Higher levels of the acceptance of suffering are found in those who prefer suffering to pleasure, as we see in the case of Saint Paul, who preferred suffering for Christ to anything else in order to bring the good news of salvation in Jesus Christ to as many people as possible. We also find this in the lives of some of the saints, like Saint Teresa of Avila and Saint John of the Cross. This is the result of special graces from God and much practice of asceticism. The highest level of the acceptance of suffering is to offer oneself as a victim to God in order to gain graces for the salvation of sinners. Only those who are specially called by God can reach this level. Examples of victim souls are Saint Thérèse of Lisieux and Saint Gemma Galgani.[4]

Suffering is an essential part of every human life. Therefore, it is unavoidable and modern medicine will never eliminate it completely. Suffering is the result of the misuse of freedom, which is what we mean by sin. The Christian should know how to deal with suffering. Jesus Christ our Savior suffered in order to save us from hell and the power of Satan. The Christian accepts suffering as the will of God and offers it up to God in reparation for his sins and the sins of the world. He does this in imitation of Jesus Christ, and in union with him. If through prayer and self-denial we can make the salvific meaning of suffering our own, we will be able to see some meaning to our suffering, and use it to attain an eternal reward with Jesus Christ and all the angels and saints.

[4] This section is based on Jordan Aumann, O.P., *Spiritual Theology* (Huntington, Ind.: Our Sunday Visitor, 1980), pp. 173–75.

12

Predestination and the Will of God

For ever, O LORD, your *word*
  is firmly fixed in the heavens.
Your faithfulness endures to all generations;
  you have established the earth, and it stands fast.
By your appointment they stand this day;
  for all things are your servants.
If your *law* had not been my delight,
  I should have perished in my affliction.
I will never forget your *precepts*;
  for by them you have given me life.
I am yours, save me;
  for I have sought your *precepts*.
The wicked lie in wait to destroy me;
  but I consider your *testimonies*.
I have seen a limit to all perfection,
  but your *commandment* is exceedingly broad.

—Psalm 119:89–96 XII (*Lamed*)

One of the most difficult problems in our Catholic faith and the teaching of the Church is the question of predestination. To "destine" someone or something means to send it to some place. The "pre" is a Latin prefix which means "before". According to Saint

Thomas Aquinas, predestination is "a plan existing in the divine mind for the ordering of some persons to eternal salvation."[1] Saint Thomas also says that predestination is a part of divine providence, which we have already considered. So predestination is the foreknowledge that God has, because of his omniscience, regarding all those who will get to heaven. He also knows all those who will be lost and go to hell because they die in the state of mortal sin. In addition, God's will is a part of predestination because God freely elects or chooses from all eternity those who will be saved. God does not destine for perdition those who are lost; he offers them the grace to be saved, but he allows them to fall into mortal sin and to die in that state without repentance. The problem here is how to reconcile God's predilection for a select group with his will to save all mankind (see 1 Tim 2:4; Rom 8:30).[2]

The Church's teaching on grace is an essential part of the notion of predestination. Here we must keep in mind several truths: (1) God loves everything he has created, especially his rational creatures. Also Saint Paul tells us in 1 Timothy 2:4 that God desires the salvation of all men, and that all come to a knowledge of the truth. Therefore God predestines no one to evil. (2) Man has free will and so he can obey God's

[1] *STh* I, 23, 2.
[2] See *New Catholic Encyclopedia* (1967), vol. 11, s.v. "Predestination in Catholic Theology".

law or reject it. (3) Christ died for all, not just for the faithful. (4) God has raised man to a supernatural end, and so man needs supernatural help or grace in order to attain it. (5) Each person receives sufficient grace to be saved, but some reject it and refuse to convert. For God's own mysterious reasons he allows this to happen; why this is so is hidden from us and so has not been revealed.[3] Why God gives efficacious grace to some and not to others is a mystery hidden in the divine will. The best answer to this difficult question was given by Saint Augustine, who said that "the judgments of God are inscrutable" (*inscrutabilia sunt iudicia Dei*).[4]

Predestination to glory is wholly gratuitous; God does not owe it to anyone, nor can anyone by his natural powers and virtues merit it. Those who do merit heaven do so because of the grace that they have received from God and their cooperation with that grace. Theologians call this type of grace "efficacious" because it is accepted and acted upon by the one who receives it.

It is important to understand that God, because of his goodness, does not predestine anyone to hell. He desires all to be saved antecedently, that is, he loves all and offers all the grace to be saved. Here we encounter the mystery of free will. God made man free, and he will not violate that freedom. Plants and animals

[3] Ibid., 716.
[4] *New Catholic Encyclopedia*, vol. 12, s.v. "Predestination".

do not have that freedom; only man on this earth enjoys freedom of the will. So God allows some men to reject him and to remain sinners, and if they die in that state they will be lost. He knows from all eternity that this will happen, but he does not will their sin or their condemnation. What God wills is the existence of free will, so that some creatures will glorify him freely; that being the case, some of those who have free will may misuse it, as some of the angels did, as Adam and Eve did, and as all sinners do. Saint Thomas says that one way to understand this is to remember that God has care of the whole universe, everything he has created, including the angels. In the context of the whole universe God wills certain defects for the good of the whole. Thus lions eat other animals, and big fish eat little fish; some men freely reject God and his law, and so are justly punished by not attaining the end for which they were created, namely, the face-to-face vision of God in heaven. God allows this to happen in order to have the good of free persons who can love God and glorify him without being forced to do it, as the plants and animals are forced by their natures.

On the other hand, it is clear from Scripture and the teaching of the Church that God positively wills the salvation of some men. He has given them a supernatural end, and he gives them the grace necessary to attain that end; on their part, they freely cooperate with God and follow his will, as Mary of Nazareth did when she said her *fiat* to the angel Gabriel at the

Annunciation. This is called positive predestination. This is brought about by the efficacious grace of God, which works together with the human intellect and will to lead man to a life of virtue as a "new creature" in sanctifying grace. Faithful Christians in this state are children of God and heirs of heaven. Included in the notion of positive predestination is the granting of the unique grace of final perseverance, so that the individual dies a happy death in the state of sanctifying grace. Such a person will go straight to heaven, or to purgatory for a time if he has temporal punishment for forgiven sins that must be endured before entering into the presence of God.

God's plan of predestination is immutable, that is, it cannot be changed. He knows from all eternity who will be saved and who will be lost. But his knowledge is not limited like our knowledge. He knows absolutely everything—past, present, and future; he also knows what would happen if individuals made different choices. It follows from this that God knows the exact number and names of those who will be saved.[5] It is important to remember here that God's foreknowledge of predestination does not *cause* those who are lost to be damned. God does not will positively the damnation of anyone. The lost freely reject God's grace and separate themselves from him for their own selfish reasons. Their guilt and damnation comes from them, not from the loving God; they

[5] *STh* I, 23, 6 and 7.

freely choose to abandon him—he does not abandon them.

In the seventeenth century there was a famous
theological debate between the Jesuits and the
Dominicans. It had to do with how God knows who
will be saved and who will be damned because of
man's exercise of free will. Any solution to the problem must respect the following truths: God's omniscience and omnipotence, and man's free will. The
Jesuit solution emphasizes man's freedom and seems
to limit God's omnipotence by making him dependent in some way on human free choice. The Domin-
ican solution emphasizes God's omniscience and
omnipotence and seems to imply a denial of man's
freedom under the influence of grace. These points
were argued before popes in the Vatican with great
fanfare. The debate had to do with the nature of
divine grace and how it influences the human free
will without violating its freedom. Neither side won
the debate. In 1607, Pope Paul V decided that both
opinions could be safely held until the Magisterium
should decide it one way or the other. That still stands,
since the Church has never resolved this question.

As was stated above, predestination to glory is a part
of divine providence, and God's foreknowledge is absolutely certain. As in many questions dealing with God,
we know certain facts, but we do not know *how* they
were produced. This is true of the Holy Trinity, the
Incarnation, Transubstantiation during the Mass, and
the influence of actual grace on the free will of man.

Regarding predestination to glory, individual persons do not know whether or not they are included in the number of the saved. Even Saint Paul said that we must work out our salvation in fear and trembling (see Phil 2:12–13). The official teaching of the Church on this point is that only those who have received a divine revelation know for certain that they are among the number of the elect. The Council of Trent said on this point: "For it is impossible, without a special revelation, to know whom God has chosen as his own." [6] A clear case of revelation regarding one's salvation is that of the good thief crucified with Jesus, to whom Jesus said, "Truly, I say to you, today you will be with me in Paradise" (Lk 23:43). It has been revealed to some of the saints, but not many, that they are among the number of the predestined. The Blessed Virgin Mary revealed to the children at Fatima that they would be taken to heaven: Jacinta and Francisco soon, as children, and Lucia later, as an adult.

With regard to predestination, the Bible refers to this divine foreknowledge as "the Book of Life". It is a metaphor referring to God's knowledge of those who will attain eternal glory (see Rev 3:5; Ps 69:28). When the Bible speaks about someone being "blotted out" of the Book of Life, it does not mean God changes his mind about someone. That is impossible. It means God knows that a person who has the grace of God,

---

[6] Denzinger-Schönmetzer, *Enchiridion Symbolorum* (Freiburg in Breisgau: Herder, 1965), 1540; see also 1565 and 1566.

and so is destined for heaven, has committed a mortal sin and will die with that sin on his soul. Such persons are only conditionally in the Book of Life, and God knows that from all eternity.

Since it is very rare for God to reveal to someone that he is predestined to eternal life, we might ask: Are there any signs in this life of being predestined to glory, of having one's name written in the Book of Life? There are certain signs of predestination; they do not offer absolute certitude, because man always remains free and can always fall into mortal sin and lose the grace of God. These signs, however, offer moral certitude that one will attain heaven. Authors of books on spirituality offer the following as signs of predestination: daily prayer; regular attendance at Mass on Sundays and Holy Days; frequent reception of the sacraments, especially Holy Communion and penance; purity of heart; keeping the Ten Commandments; love of Christ and his Church; daily recitation of the Rosary; and devotion to the Sacred Heart of Jesus and his Blessed Mother. Some would add to this the habit of spending ten or fifteen minutes a day reading the Bible. Catholics who follow a program like this have moral certitude that they will triumph over their own sensuality, overcome temptations from the world and the devil, and die in the state of sanctifying grace and so merit heaven and eternal life. This is brought about by the great grace of "final perseverance" and is what the Church means by a "happy death".

When in the Our Father we pray, "Thy will be done on earth as it is in heaven", we are asking for the grace, for ourselves and for others, to obey God's will in all things so that our names may be inscribed in "the Book of Life".

13

Love and the Will of God

Oh, how I love your *law*!
  It is my meditation all the day.
Your *commandment* makes me wiser than my enemies,
  for it is ever with me.
I have more understanding than all my teachers,
  for your *testimonies* are my meditation.
I understand more than the aged,
  for I keep your *precepts*.
I hold back my feet from every evil way,
  in order to keep your *word*.
I do not turn aside from your *ordinances*,
  for you have taught me.
How sweet are your *words* to my taste,
  sweeter than honey to my mouth!
Through your *precepts* I get understanding;
  therefore I hate every false way.

—Psalm 119:97–104 XIII (*Mem*)

The apostle John says in his first letter that God is love (4:16). This means that the nature or essence of God is love. And what do we mean by love? The word has taken on many different meanings in modern America. In these chapters we are concerned with its meaning in the Bible, in Catholic theology, and in Catholic spirituality. In the Catholic tradition, to love someone means to will good for that person; it means to affirm another. This is especially true for God because his will is identified with his own goodness. He loves his own goodness with an infinite love. Therefore he affirms his own goodness as the primary object of his will. That is why Saint John says that God is love. Since God is love, it follows that everything he does, for example in the creation of the world, is an act of love. Thus, each person exists because God loved him into existence. Since God is infinite perfection, everything he does is perfect.

In the terms of trinitarian theology, love is appropriated to the Holy Spirit, who proceeds from the Father and the Son and is the love between the Father and the Son. In Tradition he has been referred to as the "kiss" between the Father and the Son. Since the will of God is identified with the goodness of God, it follows that everything God wills is good. Thus, when God finished creating the world, he saw that it was good: "And God saw everything that he had made, and behold, it was very good" (Gen 1:31). So everything God does and everything he creates is good.

Sun, moon, stars, and all natural things praise God for his goodness (see Dan 3:35–68). They praise him naturally and necessarily by being what they are because they do not enjoy personal freedom as man does. When God created Adam and Eve he raised them to the supernatural level and established as their purpose of existence that they should have the Beatific Vision and praise God for all eternity. That is the destiny and purpose of every man and woman. But God created man in his own image and likeness, and so endowed him with intellect and will. This means that man is free to strive for his end, and free to embrace or reject God's commandments and other directions on how to attain his end.

God has manifested his will to man in the natural order by the natural law. This is accessible by reason, but in man's fallen state many people do not fully comprehend what nature requires of them. In order to make up for this, God has revealed his will to mankind by the revelation to Moses and others in the Old Testament, and especially by the revelation of Jesus Christ, the Word of God, in the New Testament. Jesus summed up the law and the prophets when he said: "You shall love the Lord your God with all your heart, and with all your soul, and with all your mind. This is the great and first commandment. And a second is like it, You shall love your neighbor as yourself. On these two commandments depend all the law and the prophets" (Mt 22:37–40).

To love God like that implies that the lover is totally one in mind and heart with the one loved. It is God's will that man keep the commandments, that he love his neighbor, that he strive for perfection, and that therefore he avoid all sinful thoughts, words, or deeds, since whatever is contrary to the holy will of God is sinful. In addition to the commandments, other manifestations of the will of God also are counsels, such as poverty and chastity, and inspirations to do some good works, such as almsgiving and visiting the sick.

God loves man and wants man to love him in return. In the Bible this mutual love is likened to the love between a husband and his wife; it is a type of "marriage" between God and the soul (see Eph 5:21–31; Song of Solomon). God invites man to love him in return, but he does not force him because love cannot be forced; it must be free.

Theologians make a distinction between the love of concupiscence and the love of friendship. The former means that I love someone for the benefit I can get out of it; it is also called a love of utility. Love of friendship, however, is also called the love of benevolence, meaning that I love someone because of his goodness and I wish good for that person. That is the kind of love that God has for man. The lover in this sense will make many sacrifices for the good of the other. We see this in the case of many parents who sacrifice their own good for the sake of their children, for example, the parents who help pay their children's college tuition, or the mother of a sick child who stays up all night in order to comfort him and take care of his needs.

Christian love is also called "charity". Charity means love of God for his own sake, and love of neighbor for the sake of God. We love our neighbor because God loves him and destined him for himself. In fact, Jesus identified himself with the neighbor as he makes clear in the parable about the Last Judgment in Matthew 25:31–46. Those on the right are saved because they served Jesus in their neighbor; those on the left are condemned because they refused to aid their neighbor in need, and in doing that did not help the Lord Jesus. The one who got it right was the Good Samaritan (Lk 10:29–37).

The subject of love is the human will, and the object is another person. When we talk about love for God, we mean that the human will wishes good to God, who is an infinite Person and is his Creator, and so wishes to be in a relation of friendship with God. God desires all men to be saved, to attain the joy of heaven. When a man loves God he unites his will with the will of God; he conforms his will to the will of God. When a person does that, then he strives to obey God in all things by keeping the commandments and by trying to avoid all venial sins and imperfections. The reason for this is that God hates sin and everything that is contrary to his will. The just man, the holy man, like Saint Joseph, is the man who obeys God in all things, avoids all deliberate sin, and lives in a union of love with God. God is absolute goodness and perfection, so the more a man becomes like God the more he shares in the goodness and perfection of God. The ultimate goal or destiny for each human person is to be united in the love of friendship with the Holy Trinity. That is what God made us for and that is what each person is really striving for, whether he knows it or not. Perfect happiness cannot be obtained in this life because everything changes and man's life is finally terminated by death. The life of man is threescore and ten, and for those who are strong fourscore (Ps 90:10).

Love for God, or charity, is a supernatural virtue that is infused into the Christian at baptism, along with faith and hope. So love in this sense is a gift from God; it is not produced by human effort, even though man can know something about God and honor him on the basis of human reason. Saint Paul is clear on this point: "God's love has been poured into our hearts through the Holy Spirit who has been given to us" (Rom 5:5).

There is no limit to how much a person can love God. It is believed to be Saint Bernard who said that the measure of love is that there is no measure. This means that you can never have too much love of God, just as you cannot have too much faith and too much hope. The reason for this is that God is infinitely lovable, so man, being finite, can never exhaust God's ability to be loved. In this life, our love is always imperfect; but in heaven, our love will be perfect according to the level of grace and glory we have attained by good works on earth.

The primary object of love or charity is the divine goodness in itself, the triune personal God: Father, Son, and Holy Spirit. We love our neighbor because he is loved by God, just as we are, and is destined for final union with God. Those who are enemies of God because of mortal sin or ignorance are still to be loved because they are potentially members of the Mystical

Body of Christ. Blessed Teresa of Calcutta cared for the dying Hindus in India because God loved them and because she saw Jesus in each one of them, even though they were not Christians.

True love involves union with the beloved; the two become one in mind and heart. So the very nature of love requires that one who loves God also identify with his thinking and his willing. The man who loves God wills what God wills. What God wills is no secret; it is made known to us by reason and faith. As Catholics, we have the guarantee of the infallible teaching of the Church in matters of faith and morals.

It is one thing to know God's will, and another thing to do it. When we pray the Our Father and say, "Thy will be done on earth as it is in heaven", we are asking God for the grace to fulfill his holy will; in that prayer we are asking for that grace not only for ourselves but also for others, that they also do the will of God. God wants man to be happy, and man's fulfillment and happiness is found only in doing the will of God. The very first psalm expresses that truth beautifully: "Blessed is the man who walks not in the counsel of the wicked, nor stands in the way of sinners, nor sits in the seat of scoffers; but his delight is in the law of the LORD, and on his law he meditates day and night. He is like a tree planted by streams of water, that yields its fruit in its season, and its leaf does not wither. In all that he does, he prospers" (Ps 1:1–3). The man who truly loves God does the will of God; he does not just talk about it and say that he loves

God. Saint Ignatius Loyola says in his famous *Spiritual Exercises* that love is shown not in words, but in deeds.[1] And Saint John says that if anyone says he loves God, whom he cannot see, and hates his neighbor, whom he can see, he is a liar (1 Jn 4:20).

Since God is love and man is made in the image and likeness of God, it follows that man is made for love. Love is the foundation of man's existence. The greatest happiness that one can find in this mortal life is love for another person or persons. Parents love their children. Husbands and wives love each other. True friends love each other and willingly make sacrifices for each other. The highest type of love that one can experience in this life is love of God. That love is directed to goodness, and God is infinitely good; therefore he is infinitely lovable. Also, God created us for himself so he is our final end after we "shuffle off this mortal coil", as Shakespeare said poetically. No human person can take the place of God as our final end or purpose in life; human persons are temporal, but God is eternal.

Listen to the plea of Moses to the people of Israel—a plea repeated and reaffirmed by Jesus in the Gospels and therefore directed also to each one of us: "Hear, O Israel: The LORD our God is one LORD; and you shall love the LORD your God with all your heart, and with all your soul, and with all your might" (Deut 6:4–5). Do that and you shall find peace and joy in this life, and everlasting happiness in the life to come.

---

[1] Puhl, *Spiritual Exercises*, nos. 230–37.

Finally, Saint Paul eloquently and beautifully proclaims the primacy of love of God in a way that has never been surpassed:

> If I speak in the tongues of men and of angels, but have not love, I am a noisy gong or a clanging cymbal. And if I have prophetic powers, and understand all mysteries and all knowledge, and if I have all faith, so as to remove mountains, but have not love, I am nothing. If I give away all I have, and if I deliver my body to be burned, but have not love, I gain nothing.
>
> Love is patient and kind; love is not jealous or boastful; it is not arrogant or rude. Love does not insist on its own way; it is not irritable or resentful; it does not rejoice at wrong, but rejoices in the right. Love bears all things, believes all things, hopes all things, endures all things.
>
> Love never ends; as for prophecies, they will pass away; as for tongues, they will cease; as for knowledge, it will pass away. For our knowledge is imperfect and our prophecy is imperfect; but when the perfect comes, the imperfect will pass away.... For now we see in a mirror dimly, but then face to face. Now I know in part; then I shall understand fully, even as I have been fully understood. So faith, hope, love abide, these three; but the greatest of these is love. (1 Cor 13:1–13)

14

The Church and the Will of God

Your *word* is a lamp to my feet
   and a light to my path.
I have sworn an oath and confirmed it,
   to observe your righteous *ordinances.*
I am sorely afflicted;
   give me life, O LORD, according to your *word*!
Accept my offerings of praise, O LORD,
   and teach me your *ordinances.*
I hold my life in my hand continually,
   but I do not forget your *law.*
The wicked have laid a snare for me,
   but I do not stray from your *precepts.*
Your *testimonies* are my heritage for ever;
   yes, they are the joy of my heart.
I incline my heart to perform your *statutes*
   for ever, to the end.

—Psalm 119:105–12 XIV (*Nun*)

The Catholic Church was founded by Jesus Christ on Peter and the apostles. He sent them out into the whole world to preach the gospel and to baptize all who would accept it in the name of the Father and of the Son and of the Holy Spirit (Mt 28:18–20). He promised them that he would be with them until the end of the world. Just as the Father sent him into the world, so he sent them out into the world with a message and a mission: "As the Father has sent me, even so I send you" (Jn 20:21).

Since the Church has a divine origin—since it was founded by Jesus Christ, who is both God and man— all men an obligation to become members of the Church once they know that the Church is from God and that he wants all men to be saved in and through the Church. Saint Paul states this clearly in 1 Timothy 2:4–5, where he says that God our Savior "desires all men to be saved and to come to the knowledge of the truth. For there is one God, and there is one mediator between God and men, the man Christ Jesus". Men desperately need salvation from their sins. Referring to Jesus Christ, Saint Peter says in Acts 4:12: "And there is salvation in no one else, for there is no other name under heaven given among men by which we must be saved." Salvation comes only from Christ, and Christ is the Head of the Church, which is his Body, as Saint Paul says several times (see Eph 1:22; Col 1:18; 1 Cor 12:17). The same idea was repeated by Pope John Paul II in the year 2000: "With the coming of the Saviour Jesus Christ, God has willed that the church founded by him be the instrument for the salvation of *all* humanity (cf. Acts 17:30–31)." [1]

---

[1] Congregation for the Doctrine of the Faith, Declaration "*Dominus Iesus*": On the Unicity and Salvific Universality of Jesus Christ and the Church (2000), no. 22.

In its broadest definition, the Church is the union of all the faithful in the whole world. Since the sixteenth century the Church has usually been defined as a union of human beings who are united by the profession of the same Christian faith, and by participation in the same sacraments under the direction of their lawful pastors, especially by the Vicar of Christ on earth and successor of Saint Peter, the Bishop of Rome.

The Catholic Church is a visible communion of believers in Jesus Christ. It was founded by Jesus in the Holy Land about two thousand years ago, and it has a long history. There is an unbroken series of popes, who rule the Church and preserve the unity of the Church; the series began with Saint Peter, and now Benedict XVI is his 265th successor. The Church is a perfect society with a hierarchical structure of bishops and priests. Christ has endowed his Church with authority to teach, to sanctify, and to rule or pastor the people of God. The whole purpose of it is to bring the faithful into loving union with God so that they may attain eternal life in heaven after they die. The Church has no mission in the areas of economics, politics, and other worldly affairs. Her purpose is spiritual—to help men save their souls and get to heaven.

In addition to having a visible structure, the Church also has an invisible and spiritual dimension. After his Ascension into heaven, Jesus sent the Holy Spirit upon his apostles and the others in the Upper Room on

Pentecost Sunday. The Holy Spirit is constantly present in the Church to guide her and to lead her members to holiness. Some of the Fathers of the Church say that the Holy Spirit is the "soul" of the Church. For, just as the soul gives life to the body of men, so the Holy Spirit gives spiritual life to those who believe in Jesus Christ, are baptized, and partake of the other sacraments of the Church.

Jesus established his Church on Peter and the apostles as his instrument for bringing about the salvation of mankind. All are invited to enter his Church. He told his apostles to go into the whole world and preach the gospel (Mt 28:19). The Church meets a need of each and every child of Adam, for we are all sinners and as such are separated from God, who is the essence of holiness. We are a fallen race because of the sin of Adam at the beginning and because of our own personal sins. Christ came into this world in order to restore to us what we lost in Adam. God has given us a supernatural goal or purpose in life, and we need his help, his grace, in order to reach it. Since it is supernatural, it cannot be attained by our natural powers.

It is God's will that we get to heaven. The means to do that are found in the Catholic Church with its sacraments and word of salvation in the gospel of Jesus Christ. The mission of the Church is to bring the good news of salvation in Jesus Christ to the whole world. When the whole world has been evangelized Christ will come again in glory to judge the living and the dead, as we profess in the Creed at Mass.

It is only in the Church that one can find salvation
and eternal happiness. That being the case, it is God's
will that all should belong to the Church. There is a
long tradition among popes and theologians that there
is no salvation outside of the Church. All grace of
Christ comes through the Church; therefore, anyone
who is saved, is saved in virtue of the Church, including those who have the grace of God even though
they are not visibly members of the Church. For all
grace of salvation is the grace of Jesus Christ, and it is
communicated to men through the Church in some
way—often in ways hidden from us.

The Catholic Church is the Body of Christ. Christ
is the Head and the members constitute his Body.
This is often called the "Mystical Body of Christ".
It is a body because it is visible and exists in history;
it is mystical because the Holy Spirit, who is the
soul of the Church, animates it. Pope Pius XII wrote
an encyclical letter explaining the Church's teaching
on this matter.[2] The Church also uses the image of
bridegroom and bride. In this way of speaking, Christ
is the Bridegroom, and the Church is his Bride. This
means that he loves the Church with an undying
love and will be united with her forever.

The Church of Christ has certain properties or characteristics that make it recognizable as a divine institution. Thus, the Church is indefectible, which means

[2] Pius XII, Encyclical on the Mystical Body of Christ, *Mystici Cor-
poris Christi* (1943).

that she is imperishable and will endure until the end of the world. This includes the immutability of her teaching, her structure, and her liturgy. This does not exclude the decay of parts of the Church and minor changes, such as changes in the liturgy and the development of dogma.

The Church is also infallible, which means that she cannot fall into error in matters of doctrine and morals. The basic reason for this is the constant indwelling and guidance of the Holy Spirit, who is the soul of the Church. As Jesus said, "I am with you always, to the close of the age" (Mt 28:20).

In addition, the Church is also a visible society because it is located in history—in time and space. It has a visible hierarchy and priesthood, a visible sacrifice in the liturgy, a visible head in the pope in Rome. It was founded by Jesus Christ and has a history that stretches from him to the present day. Also the Catholic Church is present in most of the countries of the world, even though its presence is still severely limited in places like China and India.

The traditional "marks" of the Church that help both Catholics and non-Catholics to recognize the true Church of Christ are that she is One, Holy, Catholic, and Apostolic. She is *one* because she professes the same faith and is united under the same authority of the pope and the bishops. She is *holy* because she is animated by the Holy Spirit and was founded by Jesus Christ, the Son of God. She is *catholic*, or universal, because she extends over the whole world, either actually or virtually. She is *apostolic* because she derives from the apostles, and preserves the teaching of the apostles and the succession in office on the part of the pope and bishops.

Because Christ, the God-man, founded the Church for the salvation of the human race, it is a necessary means of salvation for all. The Lord does more than politely suggest that men and women should belong to the Church he founded on Peter, the Rock. In order to reach eternal salvation, one must belong to the Church in some way. For Jesus told his apostles before his Ascension into heaven: "Go into all the whole world and preach the gospel to the whole creation. He who believes and is baptized will be saved; but he who does not believe will be condemned" (Mk 16:15–16).

We must be very careful, however, to understand "Outside of the Church there is no salvation" the way the Catholic Church understands it. It certainly does not mean that only those are saved who are physically baptized in the Catholic Church and remain in it until death. This is suggested by Pius IX when he speaks of those who remain "outside" the Church because of their "invincible ignorance" and are therefore not guilty in the eyes of the Lord. Those are invincibly ignorant of the necessity of the Church who have never heard the gospel or, having heard it, do not see that it logically requires their membership in the Holy Catholic Church.

For those who are truly invincibly ignorant, actual membership in the Church can be replaced by a desire or longing for the Church in the sense that the individual wants to do the will of God. We find this desire *explicitly* present in catechumens who are seeking baptism. But it is also *implicitly* present in all those who are faithfully trying to carry out the will of God for them to the best of their ability. In this way even those who are in fact outside the visible Catholic Church can achieve eternal salvation.

The maxim "Outside the Church there is no salvation" must be reconciled with the revealed truth that God desires the salvation of all men (see 1 Tim 2:4). Accordingly, the recent Magisterium has softened the apparent rigor of the maxim by declaring that one can be saved outside the Church by reason of his subjective disposition and good faith, and also of his unconscious desire and connection with the Church. This position was expressed by Pius IX, by Pius XII in his encyclical letter on the Mystical Body, and by the Holy Office in the Leonard Feeney case.

The full sense of the maxim, therefore, implies the following: (1) since the Church is the Mystical Body of Christ, all the means of salvation are found only in the Church, and so only in the Church are men and women regularly and commonly saved;[3] (2) all means of salvation *belong* to the Catholic Church, even those that are found accidentally outside the social structure of the Church, such as, for example, Holy Scripture,

---

[3] See Vatican II, Decree on Ecumenism (*Unitatis Redintegratio*), no. 3.

baptism, Eucharist;[4] (3) therefore, all those who are supernaturally helped by God and all those who are saved outside the Catholic Church belong in one way or another to her and are connected with her at least by an implicit desire.[5]

By admitting that non-Catholics in good faith, in virtue of their connection with or desire for the true Church, can be and are saved, the Church has not fallen into religious indifferentism or what Pope Benedict XVI refers to as "relativism". As shown in the writings of Pope Pius XII and in the documents of Vatican II, her understanding has developed with regard to the influence of God's grace on all mankind. According to God's will, therefore, membership in the Catholic Church, which is the Body of Christ, is the normal means of salvation. Those who are saved who are not members of the Church are saved through the grace of Jesus Christ that comes to them from the Church. How God does this has not been revealed to us. But the infinite mercy of God is not limited by the visible structure of the Church. The prophet Isaiah expresses this thought beautifully: "My thoughts are not your thoughts, neither are your ways my ways, says the LORD" (Is 55:8).

---

[4] See Vatican II, Dogmatic Constitution on the Church (*Lumen Gentium*), no. 8.

[5] Ibid., no. 15; also, see Pius XII, "The Letter of the Holy Office to the Archbishop of Boston", re Father Leonard Feeney, in Denzinger-Schönmetzer, 3870.

15

Prayer and the Will of God

I hate double-minded men,
  but I love your *law*.
Your are my hiding place and my shield;
  I hope in your *word*.
Depart from me, you evildoers,
  that I may keep the *commandments* of my God.
Uphold me according to your *promise*, that I may live,
  and let me not be put to shame in my hope!
Hold me up, that I may be safe
  and have regard for your *statutes* continually!
You spurn all who go astray from thy *statutes*;
  yea, their cunning is in vain.
All the wicked of the earth you count as dross;
  therefore I love your *testimonies*.
My flesh trembles for fear of you,
  and I am afraid of your *judgments*.

—Psalm 119:113–20 XV (*Samech*)

The Bible is God's word. It is a collection of love letters from God to man. An essential part of the Bible is the prayers that it contains—there are hundreds of them. Most of the noble characters in the Bible are men and women of prayer. They all pray:

Abraham, Moses, Joshua, David, the prophets, Ruth, Esther, Judith. Jesus is the supreme model of prayer, and Saints Peter and Paul imitate him. So in a certain sense the Bible is a book of prayer. The Divine Office, now called the Liturgy of the Hours, which must be prayed daily by priests and religious, is a collection of psalms, prayers, and readings taken from the Bible.

The main activity of the Catholic Church is daily prayer to God in the Sacrifice of the Mass, in the sacraments, and in the Divine Office. The reason for this is that it is God's will that we pray, and that we pray continually. Jesus himself told his disciples "always to pray and not lose heart" (Lk 18:1). Saint Paul urged the Thessalonians to "pray constantly" (1 Thess 5:17). In the Gospels Jesus is a model of prayer. He often spent the whole night in prayer to his Father; he prayed before choosing his twelve apostles; he prayed in the Garden of Gethsemane; in agony on the Cross he prayed for his enemies, "Father, forgive them; for they know not what they do" (Lk 23:34). Anyone familiar with the Bible knows how important prayer is in the lives of the main persons in the history of salvation.

Because of the importance of prayer in the life of a Christian, there are hundreds of books about how to pray and the different kinds of prayer. One of the most common definitions of prayer is that it is the "raising of the mind and heart to God." Some authors speak of it as "familiar conversation with God." Still others say that it is "spending time with the Lord" and "listening to God and responding to him." Blessed Columba Marmion defines prayer as "a conversation of a child of God with its Father in heaven under the action of the Holy Spirit." [1] In his writings he emphasizes the truth that we are adopted children of God.

All the material things below man, such as minerals, plants, and animals, do not pray because they are not free, intelligent persons. They praise God and glorify him by being what they are. This truth is stressed in some of the psalms and in the canticle of the three youths in the fiery furnace in the book of Daniel (3:57–88). Man must pray because he needs God's help and his grace in order to attain the end that God has established for him; unlike natural things, man freely moves himself to the end that God has established for him. He is free to obey God's will or to reject it. That end being supernatural, man cannot attain it by his natural talents; he needs supernatural virtues and the grace of God in order to become what God wants him to be. Only God can give man that help and that grace. In his providence he has laid it down that he will grant many graces and gifts only on condition that we ask for them[2]— hence, the necessity of the prayer of petition, which is one of the main types of prayer.

---

[1] Columba Marmion, *Christ, the Life of the Soul* (Bethesda, Md.: Zaccheus Press, 2005), p. 417.

[2] *STh* II–II, 83, 2 ad 3.

Prayer is conversation with God, with our Father who is in heaven. There is *vocal* prayer and *mental* prayer. Both types of prayer, in order to be efficacious, require attention to what one is doing. The most perfect vocal prayer is the Our Father, because it was given to us by God himself and contains everything that is essential to any prayer. In reciting vocal prayers one should pay attention to the meaning of the words; the sentiments expressed should come from the heart. Mental prayer means thinking about God and his goodness, and making acts of faith, hope, love, adoration, and thanksgiving.

In order to pray well, certain attitudes are required. The main ones are that when one prays he should be aware of the presence of God. When we speak to another person we have to be in his presence in some way—either physically or by a letter or by the telephone. In the presence of God one should show reverence for him; we do this by kneeling or taking a posture that is suitable for conversation with God and being aware of God's presence. God is our Creator, and we are creatures totally dependent on him; therefore, one should approach God in prayer with humility and recognition of our needfulness. He is infinite; he is everything. We are poor little creatures totally dependent on him and his love for us. Thoughts like these should plant some sense of humility in us and in our dealings with the Almighty. Another aspect of prayer is perseverance. Often we do not get what we ask for, so it is essential to be persistent—to persevere in prayer like the widow who pestered the judge for justice until she got what she wanted (Lk 18:2–8). The Gentile woman near Tyre asked Jesus to cure her daughter and persisted until she got what she wanted (Mk 7:24–30). There are many other examples of this in Holy Scripture.

Some prayer is absolutely necessary in order to obtain the grace of God and to save one's soul; it might even be a short prayer like "Jesus, I trust in you." It is God's will that we pray. Jesus himself told his disciples that "they ought always to pray and not to lose heart" (Lk 18:1).

In the famous Sermon on the Mount Jesus teaches us to pray constantly and insistently: "Ask, and it will be given you; seek, and you will find; knock, and it will be opened to you. For every one who asks receives, and he who seeks finds, and to him who knocks it will be opened" (Mt 7:7–8). During his Agony in the Garden, when he found Peter, James, and John sleeping, he said to them: "Watch and pray that you may not enter into temptation; the spirit indeed is willing, but the flesh is weak" (Mt 26:41).

Saint Paul imitated the Lord Jesus. His letters contain many prayers and exhortations to pray. He told the Thessalonians "pray constantly" (1 Thess 5:17). To the Colossians he wrote: "[W]e have not ceased to pray for you, asking that you may be filled with the knowledge of his will in all spiritual wisdom and understanding" (1:9).

Man is a frail and needy creature. We have bodily needs and spiritual needs. God is infinite goodness and being; he can do all things, for nothing is impossible for God. Because he is a good and loving God, we are confident that he will respond to our prayers. As we see in the Bible, prayers can be divided into prayers of worship and prayers of petition. Both are common, but the prayer of petition seems to be dominant. Most people, when they think of prayer, think about asking God for his help. The Our Father, given to us by Jesus himself, follows this pattern. The first three petitions have to do with the worship of God: *hallowed be thy name, thy kingdom come, thy will be done on earth as it is in heaven.* The last four petitions—*give us this day our daily bread, forgive us our trespasses, lead us not into temptation,* and *deliver us from evil*—have to do with man's needs, both bodily and spiritual.

Since God knows everything it is obvious that he already knows our needs. Therefore, why ask him for help? The answer to this question is that, in his providence, God has disposed things in such a way that it is his will to grant many things only on the condition that we ask for them. As Jesus said, ask and you shall receive. So if we do not ask, we will not receive. This offers us a strong motive to present our needs daily to our heavenly Father. It is his will that we ask him for what we need. If we ask unwisely, however, God will not respond. Many pray to win millions of dollars in the local lottery. Their prayer is not answered because winning the lottery may lead a person away from God and contribute to his damnation. So God sees that some of the things we ask for are not good for us with regard to attaining our final end in heaven.[3]

All sincere prayers are answered in some way, but often in ways that we are not aware of. Often God responds by giving us more than we ask for. Regular prayer increases faith, hope, and charity. It disposes the soul to receive divine blessings. Asking God for blessings is an act of humility, and it reminds us that we are mere creatures and are totally dependent on God. Prayer protects us from the power of the devil and moves us in the direction of leading a life of virtue—to practice love of God and neighbor in our daily lives.

Our prayer should not be exclusively a prayer of petition. Other forms of prayer are adoration of God, prayers to make satisfaction for past sins, and the prayer of thanksgiving. Thanks and praise of God should be included in our daily prayers. God is showering his gifts on us every minute of every hour of every day. We acknowledge this by thanking him over and over again. Every benefactor appreciates an expression of thanks; that holds for God too. Thus, many of the psalms in the Bible are prayers of praise and thanksgiving to Almighty God.

Saint Thomas Aquinas has some insightful things to say about prayer in his famous *Summa Theologiae* in

[3] For more information on prayer see "Part IV: The Lord's Prayer", in the *Catechism of the Council of Trent* (Fort Collins, Colo.: Roman Catholic Books), pp. 477–89.

the Secunda Secundae, question 83, articles 1–17. There he says that God showers us with his gifts, but some things he gives only if we ask him for them. Why is that? Saint Thomas says: "For the sake of our own good, namely, that we may acquire confidence in having recourse to God, and that we may recognize Him as the Author of our goods." [4] He also defends the propriety of asking God for temporal and material things, such as food, clothing, housing, health, and so forth. Saint Thomas, quoting from Saint Augustine, says on this point that, since it is lawful to desire temporal things since we need them in order to live, "it is lawful to pray for what it is lawful to desire." [5]

Our Lord tells us to pray always, and so does Saint Paul, but that is difficult for us because of our weakness in mind and body. Here Saint Thomas makes an important distinction between *attention* and *intention*. When we are engaged in formal prayer, it is important to give attention to what we are doing; we should be reverent and aware of the fact that we are talking to God Almighty, our Creator. We pay attention in prayer when we say the right words and attend to the meaning of the words, such as praying the Our Father or the Hail Mary. Also we should pay attention to what we are praying for.

The notion of intention has to do with praying continually, which is necessary for one striving for union

[4] *STh* II–II, 83, 2 ad 3.
[5] *STh* II–II, 83, 6.

with God. Jesus recommended it to his disciples, saying that "they ought always to pray and not lose heart" (Lk 18:1). Saint Thomas says that prayer in itself cannot be continual because we have to be busy about other works; the mind gets tired, and we need rest and recreation. But if we consider prayer in its cause, it is a different matter. On this point Saint Thomas says: "The cause of prayer is the desire of charity, from which prayer ought to arise: and this desire ought to be in us continually, either actually or virtually, for the virtue of this desire remains in whatever we do out of charity." [6] So we are praying continually if we make the intention of offering to God all of our prayers, works, joys, and sufferings of each day as we do the Morning Offering. There is much merit in this for eternal life, and the Church urges all of us to pray the Morning Offering daily.

God made me to know him, love him, and serve him in this life, and to be happy with him forever in the next life. In order to reach that goal, I have to do God's will for me. It is a long, hard road, and it requires perseverance. I need God's help, and he is always there to help me. Many things he gives me only if I pray for them. So it is God's will that I pray, and pray continually. Father Joseph-Marie Perrin, O.P., says on this point that "life becomes a prayer if it is lived in God's will." [7]

---

[6] *STh* II–II, 83, 14.

[7] Joseph-Marie Perrin, O.P., *The Little Manual of Perfect Prayer & Adoration* (Manchester, N.H.: Sophia Institute Press, 2002), p. 169.

16

Death and the Will of God

I have done what is just and right;
  do not leave me to my oppressors.
Be surety for your servant for good;
  let not the godless oppress me.
My eyes fail with watching for your salvation,
  and for the fulfilment of your righteous *promise*.
Deal with your servant according to your steadfast love,
  and teach me your *statutes*.
I am your servant; give me understanding,
  that I may know your *testimonies*!
It is time for the LORD to act,
  for your *law* has been broken.
Therefore I love your *commandments*
  above gold, above fine gold.
Therefore I direct my steps by all your *precepts*;
  I hate every false way.

—Psalm 119:121–28 XVI (*Ayin*)

Life is a gift from God. In the beginning God created the heavens and the earth and everything on it,
including plants, animals, and man. All living material things are composed of parts which in time
are separated; when they come apart, they die. This

happens to all living things on this earth, including man. But life is a problem for intelligent beings like man. He wants to hold on to life; he wants to live forever, but he is threatened with death every day from the moment of his birth. Death follows man like a shadow—there is no escape. It can come suddenly, because of an automobile accident, or being struck by lightning, or a heart attack. Nevertheless, man instinctively feels that there is something wrong about death, that it should not be, that he should not have to die. Death seems to mean the dissolution of man's personal existence; perhaps that is the reason why most men fear death and will do almost anything to avoid it.

Since existence is good and all things strive for what is good, all living things strive to preserve themselves in life. This is especially true of man. Man is by nature mortal, but his first parents, Adam and Eve, were created immortal by God as we read in Genesis 2 and 3. God endowed man in Paradise with the preternatural gift of bodily immortality. Thus, in their original state Adam and Eve were exempted from the law of death. As a punishment for their disobedience, however, they were made subject to the death that God had warned them about. For God had said: "[O]f the tree of the knowledge of good and evil you shall not eat, for in the day that you eat of it you shall die" (Gen 2:17). And in the next chapter we read: "In the sweat of your face you shall eat bread till you return to the ground, for out of it you were taken; you are dust, and to dust you shall return" (3:19). Every year on Ash Wednesday the Church reminds us of the fact of our mortality when the priest puts ashes on our foreheads while pronouncing those unforgettable words.

Saint Paul teaches that death is a result of Adam's sin. "[A]s sin came into the world through one man and death through sin, and so death spread to all men because all men sinned" (Rom 5:12). On this point the Council of Trent said that death is a punishment for sin.[1] But for those who die in the state of sanctifying grace death is not so much a punishment as it is a consequence of sin. Since our Lord and his Blessed Mother were free from original sin and all personal sin, death for them was not a result of sin; it was rather a consequence of life in a material body.

According to Genesis, Saint Paul and the Council of Trent, all human beings, as descendants of Adam and Eve, are subject to original sin (except Jesus and Mary); therefore, they are all subject to the law of death. The key biblical text for this is Romans 5:12–21. Saint Paul also says in Hebrews 9:27, "[I]t is appointed for men to die once, and after that comes judgment."[2]

God did not bring about death; man did, in Adam. God created man with immortality. The book of Wisdom says that "God did not make death, and he does not delight in the death of the living" (Wis 1:13).

---

[1] Denzinger-Schönmetzer, *Enchiridion Symbolorum*, 1511.

[2] Gen 1–3, Rom 5:12–21; Council of Trent, DS 1510–14.

Further on the sacred author says that "God created man for incorruption . . . but through the devil's envy death entered the world" (2:23–24). So death entered into the world because our first parents, following the suggestion of Satan, violated the express will of God, even after he had warned them that they would die if they ate the forbidden fruit.

The reality of death for all human beings is absolutely certain, but the time of death is uncertain. We all know that we will die, but we do not know when it will happen. Man is here today and gone tomorrow. There is an old saying that two things in life are certain—death and taxes. Some may be able to escape taxes, but no one can escape death.

People do not like to talk about death because they do not want to be reminded of it. When a relative or friend dies, they often use euphemisms like he "passed away" or "left us" or "kicked the bucket" in order to avoid using the word "death". Every day the media report on killings and people dying, but they do not offer any comments on the meaning of death. For most people, especially those without faith in Jesus Christ, the subject is too painful.

All fear death and try to avoid it any way they can. Old people spend much of their time and money trying to delay the inevitability of death. They fear the suffering involved in death, but they fear even more what will happen to them after they have died. How will God judge them? Will they go to heaven or to hell? And what about the prospect of purgatory for those who are saved but still must make satisfaction for the sins they have committed? Because death means entering into a world that is unknown, man fears it and tries to avoid it.

The definition of death on the physical level is that it is the separation of the soul, the principle of life, from the body of a living being. There are certain signs of death: cessation of breathing and movement of the limbs, coldness to the touch, and after some time, decomposition, during which the body falls apart. It returns to the dust from which it was taken.

Death means corruption of the body, but what happens to the soul? What happens to my personal existence and my consciousness of who I am? As Christians we know that the soul is immortal, that it lives on after it is separated from the body. But what that life is like we do not know. In the Gospels Jesus speaks about heaven and hell as the permanent dwelling place of those who are saved and those who are condemned. That is made clear in the parable of the rich man and Lazarus in Luke 16:19–31. Most people, and rightly so, are very concerned about what will happen to them after they die.

Because of divine revelation and the teaching of the Church, Catholics know that after death the soul goes to purgatory for a time if it must be purified, and to heaven or hell forever. So there are really only two final possibilities—heaven or hell. Implied in these two possibilities is the fact that a judgment will be made, as Saint Paul says in Hebrews 9:27. The Catholic Church refers to the judgment immediately after death as the "particular judgment", which is to be distinguished from the General Judgment of all mankind at the end of the world, when Christ will come again in glory to judge the living and the dead. This judgment is final and irrevocable. Since God knows everything that has ever happened in the world, and everything that will happen in the future—since his knowledge is infinite—he knows perfectly the state of the soul of each person. Nothing is hidden from his eyes. He knows instantly whether the person is deserving of heaven or hell. There is no need for lawyers, and there is no appeal to a higher court. The judgment of us by Jesus after our death is the Supreme Court of Heaven, from which there is no appeal.

Most people, especially when they get older, often think about death and what it means. Death means the end of man's earthly existence in time and space. His soul, now separated from his body, enters into eternity—there is no more time for him. The time of trial, suffering, toil, and merit is over. In eternity there is no past, present, and future such as we experience in time. Eternity is the complete possession of life all at once—it is a perpetual now. Death is also irrevocable. There is no such thing as reincarnation or transmigration of souls as the pantheistic religions believe. Again, as Saint Paul says, it is appointed to men once to die, and after this the judgment. The blessed who go to heaven will be happy there forever and cannot lose it; the damned who go to hell will be there forever and cannot escape, either by a conversion of heart or by annihilation.

These truths remind us that death is a serious matter. It is much more serious than the way it is treated in our media of entertainment and daily news. In this changeable life, if one makes a mistake, he can correct it and start over again. That does not apply to those who die. You die only once—there is no second chance.

Accordingly, it is extremely important to prepare now for death. The main way of doing that is to lead a life of virtue, to obey God's Ten Commandments, to strive to do God's will at all times and in all places. This can be summed up in Jesus' basic command to love God and one's neighbor. In order to remain faithful and to overcome evil temptations, which all are subject to, it is essential to pray often, to practice some self-denial, and to be generous to those in need. Also, it is spiritually helpful to think often about death, which will surely come one day. The saints say that one should live each day as though it were his last day. Our Lord said that he will come like a thief in the night—at a time when you do not expect him.[3] Now we have the time to use these spiritual means; we have the time to ask for the grace to accept God's will regarding the time and manner of our death, and we have the time to pray for the grace of final perseverance.

---

[3] Thomas à Kempis, *The Imitation of Christ*, bk. 1, chap. 23, no. 3.

Now is the time to lay up treasures of merit in heaven by receiving the sacraments regularly, by doing good deeds, and by avoiding all sin, both mortal sin and venial sin. God made us without asking our consent, but he will not admit us to his presence without our working for it. He made us free, and he will not violate our freedom. We are free to choose either good or evil, so we should work out our salvation in fear and trembling, as Saint Paul says in Philippians 2:13. We read in *The Imitation of Christ*: "Be always prepared, and live in such a manner that death may never find thee unprovided." [4]

The prayers of the Church over a dead body in a funeral service stress begging for God's mercy and forgiveness for the dead person and granting him the gift of eternal life in heaven. The prayers presuppose the reality and certainty of eternal life—in heaven with Christ for those who die in the state of sanctifying grace, and in hell for those who die unrepentant in the state of mortal sin as enemies of God. With the Church we beseech God: "Eternal rest grant unto him, O Lord, and let perpetual light shine upon him. May his soul, and the souls of all the faithful departed, through the mercy of God rest in peace. Amen."

Because of his death and Resurrection, Jesus merited eternal life for himself and for all those who share in his life through faith and love, and divine grace, which is the supernatural life of the soul. Because he

[4] Ibid.

accepted death in an act of free submission to the will of his Father, Jesus' obedience has transformed the curse of death into a blessing.[5] Thus, because of Christ, Christian death has a positive meaning. As Saint Paul said, "The saying is sure: if we have died with him, we shall also live with him" (2 Tim 2:11). For the Christian, therefore, death is entrance into eternal life with Christ.

We Catholics are a people of hope because we live spiritually by the life of Christ. So for us death is not the end of life; it is the beginning of eternal life that no one can take away from us. Saint Thérèse of Lisieux on her deathbed said: "I am not dying; I am entering life." [6]

Because we die "in Christ", the Church prays in the Preface of Christian Death (Roman Missal): "Lord, for your faithful people life is changed, not ended. When the body of our earthly dwelling lies in death, we gain an everlasting place in heaven."

In the beginning God created man immortal. By his sin and the misuse of freedom, Adam rebelled against God and so brought death into the world for himself and all his descendants. God positively willed that man should not die, but there was one condition— that he should not eat of the tree of the knowledge of good and evil. Since God made man free, for his own mysterious reasons he permitted Adam to misuse his

[5] See *CCC* 1009.
[6] Saint Thérèse of Lisieux, *The Last Conversations*, quoted in *CCC* 1011.

freedom, to sin and so to incur the punishment of death. But in his providence he decreed that what we lost in Adam we should recover superabundantly through the Incarnation, life, death, and Resurrection of Jesus Christ, the only Son of God and the Savior of all mankind. It was the will of God that what we lost in Adam we should regain in Christ, the Second Adam.

17

Obedience and the Will of God

Your *testimonies* are wonderful;
   therefore my soul keeps them.
The unfolding of your *words* gives light;
   it imparts understanding to the simple.
With open mouth I pant,
   because I long for your *commandments*.
Turn to me and be gracious to me,
   as you always do toward those who love your name.
Keep steady my steps according to your *promise*,
   and let no iniquity get dominion over me.
Redeem me from man's oppression,
   that I may keep your *precepts*.
Make thy face shine upon your servant,
   and teach me your *statutes*.
My eyes shed streams of tears,
   because men do not keep your *law*.

—Psalm 119:129–36 XVII (*Peh*)

Obedience is an essential moral virtue. It is the king
of all the moral virtues. If Adam and Eve had been
obedient to God, the world would be completely different. There would be no suffering and death. If all
human beings just obeyed the Ten Commandments,

we would have a paradise on earth: there would be no killing, adultery, stealing, or lying. Obedience is the most important moral virtue because it submits man's most noble faculty, namely his will, to the will of another person who has lawful authority. The Christian does this out of the supernatural motive of love of God, who is infinite goodness and truth. The best way to attain happiness in this vale of tears is by uniting one's will with the will of God, because God has made man to be united with himself in love for all eternity. So embracing God's will in this life is the beginning of eternal happiness and freedom.

Obedience is defined as the moral virtue that inclines the human will to comply with the will of another who has the right and authority to command. For Christians it is also a supernatural virtue because it rests on God's almighty power as our Creator and on the submission that all creatures owe to him. God has established order in the universe. This means that the lower submits to the control of the higher. In the context of human affairs this means that God has delegated his authority to certain individuals who, as lawful superiors, create principles of unity within society. Some of these are the family, the civic community, the Church, and free associations that one might join, such as a religious order like the Benedictines or Jesuits.

Who are the lawful superiors? They are the individuals whom God recognizes as the head of various societies. In the natural order the head of the family is the father; in civil society it is the lawful rulers who hold authority. In the supernatural order lawful authority is placed in the Church, in the person of the Sovereign Pontiff, whose authority is supreme and immediate over the whole Church. Bishops then have authority over their diocese, and priests have spiritual authority from their bishop over the parishioners. In addition, there are the superiors of religious orders who get their authority from the pope; there are also diocesan congregations whose superior gets his authority from the local bishop.

God's authority over us, as our Creator, is unlimited. Human authority is limited by the nature of the society in which it is exercised. Human authorities are limited by the natural law, by the eternal law of God, and by the positive laws of their community. So subjects are not bound to obey a superior when he commands something contrary to the law of God or beyond his authority. Thus when the Jerusalem officials forbade the apostles to preach the gospel Saint Peter replied: "We must obey God rather than men" (Acts 5:29). The authority of bishops and priests is limited by canon law, and that of religious superiors is limited by the constitutions of the religious community.

There are many outstanding examples in the Bible of obedience to God and lawful authority. For example, Abraham obeyed God when he was ordered to sacrifice his only son, Isaac (Gen 22). Moses was commanded by God again and again to do various things, and he obeyed; as a result he led the chosen people out of Egypt and eventually to the Promised Land (Exodus). The prophet Samuel obeyed God and consecrated Saul as king of Israel; later, he anointed David as king in place of Saul. Saul disobeyed God, and so God rejected him (1 and 2 Samuel). The same can be said about the call of the prophets, especially Isaiah, Jeremiah, and Ezekiel.

In the New Testament there are many edifying examples of obedience to God. Mary obeyed God when she uttered her *fiat* to become the Mother of the Messiah: "Let it be done to me according to your word" (Lk 1:38). Joseph obeyed God each time he was told in a dream what to do. Jesus obeyed his heavenly Father by staying at the temple at the age of twelve; then he went to Nazareth with his parents and "was obedient to them" (Lk 2:49–51). When Jesus invited Peter and Andrew and James and John to follow him, although they were fishermen and busy with their boats, they abandoned everything and became his disciples (Mk 1:16–20). Jesus himself is a perfect example of obedience. By his obedience to his heavenly Father he worked the redemption of mankind: "For as by one man's disobedience many were made sinners, so by one man's obedience many will be made righteous" (Rom 5:19). Saint Paul makes the same point in Philippians 2:8: "And being found in human form he humbled himself and became obedient unto death, even death on a cross." Saint John says that we prove our love for our neighbor by loving God and keeping his commandments: "By this we know that we love the children of God, when we love God and obey his commandments" (1 Jn 5:2). Love for Jesus is shown by keeping his commandments: "He who has my commandments and keeps them, he it is who loves me" (Jn 14:21).

Spiritual authors and saints like Ignatius of Loyola, Teresa of Avila, John of the Cross, and Francis de Sales point out that there are various degrees or levels of obedience. The first level is that of beginners in the spiritual life, who strive to avoid mortal sin and to keep the Ten Commandments. In daily life they strive to fulfill all their serious obligations. They may find it difficult, but with the help of God's grace they try to remain in the state of sanctifying grace. The second level is that of the advanced, those who are making progress in union with God. These strive to avoid all deliberate venial sins, submitting their will to their superior. The third level is that of the perfect. They obey God and their superiors willingly, and even submit their judgment to that of the superior in all things that are not manifestly sinful.

Catholics should be obedient to higher authority in family, state, and Church because all authority comes from God. If we have the habit of seeing God in our superiors, it is much easier to be obedient. As a virtue obedience is pleasing to God because it means the sacrifice of one's will out of love of God. So the supernatural dimension of obedience is very important for those who strive for Christian perfection. This means that one should obey his lawful superior in all things.

Those who are perfect in obedience always obey promptly, perseveringly, and with a cheerful outlook. Saint Paul says that "God loves a cheerful giver" (2 Cor 9:7). If the superior commands something that is doubtful, it is not opposed to the spirit of obedience to approach the superior and ask for a clarification.

The excellence of obedience should be clear from what has been said. Saint Thomas Aquinas says that, after the virtue of religion, obedience is the most perfect of all the moral virtues because it unites us closer to God than the other virtues do. The reason is that obedience detaches us from self-will, which is the main obstacle to union with God.[1] By uniting us to God, obedience helps us to participate in the life of God. This submission also merits an increase of divine grace because it is freely made. When one is obedient, he is imitating Christ our Savior who said in his Agony in the Garden, "Father ... not my will, but yours, be done" (Lk 22:42). The sacrifice of one's will to God is the highest sacrifice that one can make; it is better than the sacrifice involved in the vow of poverty and in the vow of chastity. Poverty concerns material possessions, and chastity is the sacrifice of bodily pleasures and the love of a wife and children. Obedience means sacrificing one's own will, which is man's most precious possession. The holy author says in this regard that "to obey is better than sacrifice" (1 Sam 15:22).

---

[1] For an excellent treatment of obedience see Tanquerey, *Spiritual Life*, pp. 1068–74.

Saint Augustine spoke of obedience as the mother of all virtues because if one obeys, one will practice all the virtues. If we obey Jesus we will practice all the virtues he recommends in the Gospels, such as prayer, penance, justice, religion, generosity, and gratitude.

There are many personal rewards for being obedient to God, whether directly to him in his commandments or indirectly through his human representatives who share in the authority of God. Often people are not sure about whether or not they are doing God's will. So, when we are obedient to a legitimate superior, we know that we are doing God's will. This is especially true for priests and religious who obey their superiors; but it is also true for the laity when they are under someone's authority and do what they are told. We have the example of Jesus, who said of his Father, "I always do what is pleasing to him" (Jn 8:29).

Peace of soul is a precious gift. Those who disobey God and live in mortal sin cannot have peace of soul because they are not living as they should. The obedient person has a peaceful soul because he knows he is doing what God wants him to do; he is sharing in God's life of grace, and so he is working out his salvation. On this point the Psalmist says, "Great peace have those who love thy law" (Ps 119:165). Moreover, everything that is done in daily life—meals, sleep, prayer, study, work, recreation—if it is done out of a sense of obedience to God, is meritorious and contributes to a daily growth in grace and holiness. Also, men and women who obey God to the best of their ability are usually cheerful and hopeful persons because they know they are doing what God wants them to do and therefore have moral certainty about their eternal salvation.

There are many positive benefits and fruits of obedience to lawful authority out of reverence for God, who is the source of all authority. Disobedience is a cause of conflict and hard feelings in any community, while the obedient person generally will get along well with others, whether in the family or in some other society. Obedience also contributes to correct judgment regarding both earthly and divine things, for the obedient person in some way shares in the wisdom of God because he is following God's counsel. By the practice of perfect obedience, one remains open to the influence of the Holy Spirit and the increase of the gift of counsel. That is most advantageous especially for superiors who need divine guidance in directing and commanding others.

Another effect of obedience is that it strengthens the will. Self-will and selfishness are major obstacles to holiness and striving to be a saint. Obedience to superiors is a great aid to overcoming self-will. If one obeys from a supernatural motive of serving God, he knows that he is being directed by God and so will receive the grace he needs to fulfill the command, no matter what it might be. Saint Augustine said in this regard: "Lord, give me the strength to do what you command, and then command what you will." Thus, when a command is given, and one knows that it comes from divine authority, one knows with certainty that he will receive the grace from God to accomplish it. There are many examples of this on the part of martyrs, such as the Jesuit martyrs in Japan, who were obedient to God's will and received the grace to endure cheerfully their intense sufferings. God does not abandon those who are faithful to him.

It has been said that "To serve God is to reign", that is, to reign over one's passions, to reign over greed and selfishness, to reign over the devil and his temptations, to reign over the secular world. By obeying lawful superiors for the love of God, one participates in the life of God, and therefore in his liberty. So obedience and grace, which make us participate in the nature of God (2 Pet 1:4), make us also children of God and heirs of heaven. The love of the Holy Spirit is poured into our hearts and, as Saint Paul says, "[W]here the Spirit of the Lord is, there is freedom" (2 Cor 3:17).

In conclusion, from the above it should be obvious that obedience to the will of God, for the laity and for priests and religious, motivated by the love of God, has the effect of a peaceful, happy life on this earth and prepares us for entrance into eternal life when God calls us home.[2]

---

[2] Reginald Garrigou-Lagrange, O.P., "The Grandeur of Obedience", chap. 15 in *The Three Ages of the Spiritual Life* (Rockford, Ill.: Tan Books, 1948), 2:154–57.

18

Vocation in Life and the Will of God

You are righteous, O LORD,
  and right are your *judgments*.
You have appointed your *testimonies* in righteousness
  and all faithfulness.
My zeal consumes me,
  because my foes forget your *words*.
Your *promise* is well tried,
  and your servant loves it.
I am small and despised,
  yet I do not forget your *precepts*.
Your righteousness is righteous forever,
  and your *law* is true.
Trouble and anguish have come upon me,
  but your *commandments* are my delight.
Your *testimonies* are righteous forever;
  give me understanding that I may live.

—Psalm 119:137–44 XVIII (*Tsade*)

When God created the universe and each one of us
we can say that he called us out of nothingness and
assigned to each one of us a purpose. All material things
below man, like elements, plants, and animals, have
their purpose or end established for them by nature

and instinct. By being themselves they praise and glorify God, as we see in a beautiful red rose, a majestic racehorse, or a blazing sunset. Man, since he is intelligent and free, has many possibilities. But in his providence God has assigned a role in life for each one of us. It is up to us to discover, in the process of growing up to maturity, what God is calling us to do with our lives. The call of God is the same thing as a vocation in life.

In Catholic culture and tradition, until very recently, the word "vocation" was applied almost exclusively to those who entered the priesthood or the religious life as a monk or nun. It is only in recent years that the term has been expanded to include a vocation, or God's call, to marriage or the single life. So the word now has a general meaning of choosing, under the influence of God's grace, a permanent way of life. I think this development may be a result of the teaching of Vatican II in chapter 5 of the Dogmatic Constitution on the Church (*Lumen Gentium*), which states that all are called by God to a life of holiness; all are called to be saints. Therefore, striving to be a saint is not restricted to just priests and religious.

Our concern here is an investigation into the connection between the will of God and the vocation in the life of a man or woman. The main point is that God created each one of us for a definite purpose; the ultimate goal of all is union with God in love in heaven, and we achieve that by conforming ourselves to his will. But God does not grant heaven to us without our meriting it by leading a life of virtue. So it is up to each one of us to find out what God wants us to do with our lives. For many that seems to take place in the late teens. Others have a clear grasp of what they want to do with their life at an early age. That was the case with Saint Thérèse of Lisieux. Archbishop Fulton J. Sheen said that he knew he wanted to be a priest when he was five years old.

In general terms, we can define a vocation as a call to a person from God, in the form of a special grace, that moves or inclines him to embrace a particular way of life. Some calls from God are miraculous and leave no room for doubt, such as the call to Abraham, Moses, Isaiah, Jeremiah, Joseph, the apostles, or especially Saint Paul, who was knocked to the ground and called by the Lord Jesus (Acts 9). Blessed Mother Teresa received an inspiration while riding on a train in India that she should leave the order of nuns she belonged to and dedicate herself to caring for the poorest of the poor. It seems, though, that most people gradually develop a sense of what God wants them to do in life. Of course, there are many examples of young people who rush into a marriage without proper preparation, and later bitterly regret it.

There are many different vocations, and there are also vocations within vocations, such as a married person who is also a teacher or doctor or lawyer; many priests are also teachers or scientists. For a Catholic there are basically five different vocations to choose from: marriage, single life, priesthood, religious or consecrated life as a monk or nun, or member of a secular institute. They are all means to attain the purpose of human life, which is holiness and union with God by doing his will. We pray that we may be able to do that every time we say the Our Father, with the invocation "thy will be done on earth as it is in heaven."

God calls most Catholics to marriage and family life. Vatican II made it very clear that married persons are to strive for holiness just as priests and religious do: "It is therefore quite clear that all Christians in any state or walk of life are called to the fullness of Christian life and to the perfection of love." [1] The Council here is merely repeating what Jesus said in the Sermon on the Mount: "You, therefore, must be perfect, as your heavenly Father is perfect" (Mt 5:48). Saint Paul makes the same point: "For this is the will of God, your sanctification" (1 Thess 4:3).

Some individuals are called to the single life, or perhaps they do not marry or enter the religious life because they cannot see clearly what God wants them to do. Some seek a spouse but never find the right person. That also is a sign of God's will. In any event, they are all called to try to find the will of God in their lives and to strive for holiness.

Some members of the faithful are called by God to dedicate their life full-time to a religious way of life, either as a priest or a monk or a nun. Some of

---

[1] *Lumen Gentium*, no. 40.

the signs of such a vocation are that there are no natural or legal obstacles to the vocation in question, such as ill health or the bond of marriage. In addition, one must have certain aptitudes for a religious vocation such as adequate health, proper age, emotional stability, intellectual ability, and a good moral character. One must also have the gift of chastity and the firm resolve to live a chaste life for the kingdom of God in imitation of Jesus and Mary. No one can be forced by parents or anyone else to embrace a life of the evangelical counsels. It must be freely chosen. Of course, one may think that he has a vocation and be mistaken. Seminaries and novitiates are times of testing and trial for young people to make a final decision that God is calling them to serve him in that way. After evaluating a candidate, the bishop or religious superior may tell the individual that he is not suited and so dismiss him. This is a sign from the Church that the individual does not have a vocation, at least to that way of life. If the superior accepts a candidate, it is a sign that it is God's will, since religious superiors have their authority from God.

The evangelical counsels are just that—counsels. They are essential helps in striving for perfection, but they do not bind in conscience as the commandments do. However, if a young man or woman receives a sure inspiration to embrace the religious life and, because of sloth or some other fault, refuses to follow the invitation, it would be a sinful act. But such a refusal does not necessarily mean that the individual would lose his soul.

Very few vocations from God are as clear as that of Saint Paul on the road to Damascus. He responded to the call with his whole heart and soul, and for the rest of his life he was aware of the fact that he was called to be an apostle of Jesus Christ. Most of his letters begin with an explicit reference to his calling. Here are a few examples: "Paul, a servant of Jesus Christ, called to be an apostle, set apart for the gospel which he promised beforehand through his prophets in the holy scriptures" (Rom 1:1); "Paul, called by the will of God to be an apostle of Christ Jesus" (1 Cor 1:1); "Paul, an apostle—not from men nor through man, but through Jesus Christ and God the Father" (Gal 1:1); "Paul, an apostle of Christ Jesus by the will of God" (Eph 1:1). So God called Saint Paul to be an apostle of Jesus Christ, and Paul was always aware of the fact that he was sent and supported by the grace of Christ. Most of us do not receive that kind of call, but God does manifest his will for us by the circumstances surrounding our lives and by the influence of other persons.

The certain way to holiness and eternal salvation is to love God with one's whole heart and mind and soul. If one truly loves God he necessarily conforms himself to the will of God insofar as he knows it. But one must be sincere. The way to holiness is clearly stated in the Bible. Jesus is very blunt about this: "Not everyone who says to me, 'Lord, Lord,' shall enter the kingdom of heaven, but he who does the will of my Father who is in heaven" (Mt 7:21).

We are all moved and surrounded by the grace of God. And we should never forget that grace is totally gratuitous—that is what the word "grace" means. Since it is a gift, we ought to be aware of that fact, and we ought to thank God every day for the gifts of nature and grace that he has given us. As Catholics and Christians God has elected us for eternal life. And we will get there if we hearken to his call and do his will. Just as there are many different roads to Rome (or New York), so also there are many different roads to heaven. God loves all of his children, but he does not love all of them to the same degree. Some he loves more than others; this is obvious from the various gifts of nature and grace that he pours out on them. If some have more gifts than I have, that is no reason to protest or to be envious, because everything I have, except my own sins, is a gift from God for which I should be grateful. Don't forget our Lord's parable about the employer who hired workers at different times throughout the day and paid those who worked only one hour the same as he paid those who had worked the whole day. To those who grumbled, he said: "Take what belongs to you, and go; I choose to give to this last as I give to you. Am I not allowed to do what I choose with what belongs to me? Or do you begrudge my generosity?" (Mt 20:1–16). We should not be envious or among those who begrudge God's generosity, but rather we should rejoice in the good fortune of others because we are all members of the same family, the Mystical Body of Christ. We are blessed in the gifts that others have received, since we share in their gifts. We should rejoice and give thanks to God for the gifts of nature and grace that he has given to us.

19

Family and the Will of God

With my whole heart I cry; answer me, O LORD!
   I will keep your *statutes*.
I cry to you; save me,
   that I may observe your *testimonies*.
I rise before dawn and cry for help;
   I hope in your *words*.
My eyes are awake before the watches of the night,
   that I may meditate on your *promise*.
Hear my voice in your steadfast love;
   O LORD, in your justice preserve my life.
They draw near who persecute me with evil purpose;
   they are far from your *law*.
But you are near, O LORD,
   and all your *commandments* are true.
Long have I known from your *testimonies*
   that you have founded them forever.

— Psalm 119:145–52 XIX (*Qaf*)

At the present time in most countries in the West
the traditional family is in serious trouble. There are
many reasons for this. Surely some of the reasons
would be the growth of technology and man's control over nature; the increase of atheism, secularism,

materialism, and individualism that give primacy to the individual over God and the family; and the daily promotion of these ideas through the media of mass communication. Many say that the family is in crisis, given the high rate of divorces, abortions, and couples living together who are not married. Physician-assisted suicide is on the rise. Then there is also the increase of homosexuality and same-sex marriage, which is based on sodomy and seeks public acceptance as an alternative to marriage between a man and a woman. All of these trends have a negative effect on traditional, stable marriages and families.

In the context of meditating on the will of God I wish to point out that the marriage of one man and one woman, with the purpose of establishing a family, was established by God when in the beginning he created man male and female (Gen 1–2). Man and woman complement each other and are naturally attracted to each other. When they are joined together in a permanent bond of marriage and become "two in one flesh" in the marital embrace, they conceive and give birth to children. This community of persons we call a "family" was created by God when he made them male and female, so it is clear that the family is willed by God and is therefore a natural institution. The family was not established by man independently of the will of God. It is not a society that "evolved" from ape-like groups as the evolutionists would have it. The origin of the family is clearly explained and truthfully proclaimed in the Bible, beginning with Genesis 1–2.

The family is the most basic human society. It precedes the state both in time and in dignity. All human persons belong to a family; they are conceived by their father and mother, and born of a mother. Orphans and abandoned children might not know who their parents are, but still they have a mother and a father. (We are not considering here cloning, in vitro fertilization, surrogate motherhood, and other immoral ways of producing human beings.)

The *Catechism of the Catholic Church* gives this definition of a family: "A man and a woman united in marriage, together with their children, form a family." [1] Father John A. Hardon, S.J., says that a family is "a group of persons who are related by marriage or blood and who typically include a father, mother, and children." [2] Families, therefore, are the result of the marriage of a man and a woman who, out of love for each other, consent to live together and to have children, if it pleases God to give children to them. The marriage bond results from the free consent, given externally and publicly, between a man and a woman who have sufficient age and maturity to make a permanent commitment. A key point regarding marriage is that God established its nature and it does not depend on the subjective ideas of the persons entering into it. For example, if a man getting married thinks marriage is just a temporary arrangement, or if he

[1] *CCC* 2202.
[2] Hardon, *Modern Catholic Dictionary*, s.v. "Family", p. 206.

refuses to have any children, then there is no marriage—it is null and void. Marriage and the family is a community of love and life; it is a community of persons for life; it is a natural community whose rules have been set by God its Creator. If a couple getting married do not accept that, then they surely are not entering into a Catholic, sacramental marriage.

Two basic human drives, implanted in man by God who made him, are self-preservation and preservation of the species. The latter is accomplished morally and legitimately by the sexual union between a husband and his wife. The sex drive is an essential part of the desire to enter into marriage and found a family. This means that sex and its consequences are willed by God and are good because he created them. The sacred author tells us in Genesis 1:31: "And God saw everything that he had made, and behold, it was very good." God commanded Adam and Eve to use their sexual powers and to have children: "And God blessed them, and God said to them, 'Be fruitful and multiply, and fill the earth and subdue it'" (Gen 1:28).

In this regard it is important to remember that all human beings born into this world are composed of body and soul. The soul is immortal and is created directly by God when each child is conceived as a result of sexual union. As Catholics we know that God created man with a supernatural end, that is, he destined man for the face-to-face vision of God if he dies in the state of sanctifying grace. Seeing God face-to-face in a union of love and friendship is beyond the ability of human nature as such. This immense gift was given by God to Adam in addition to his gifts of nature but it is not a requirement of his nature; that is why it is called "supernatural". Adam lost it by his sin, but it was restored to us by Jesus Christ, the God-man, who merited eternal life for us by his sacrificial death on the Cross of Calvary two thousand years ago. That life is communicated to us through his Church and the reception of the sacraments, especially the sacrament of baptism, which makes us children of God and heirs of heaven. That life is nourished and increased by the other six sacraments, including the sacrament of holy matrimony.

Saint Augustine said that Christian marriage has three characteristics or qualities: offspring, fidelity, and sacrament. That insight has been incorporated into Church teaching for many centuries. The main purpose of matrimony is the generation of children to increase the human family and to add new souls who are destined for eternal happiness with God in heaven. This is God's way to create new immortal persons who can enjoy the Beatific Vision. The word "matrimony" indicates its purpose, since it is derived from the Latin word for mother, *mater.*

There is more to marriage than the generation of children. They must also be educated, and that takes a long time, until they are able to stand on their own and start their own families. In order to accomplish this, husband and wife are bound to each other for life—for their own good and for the good of their children. For this reason a Christian marriage between two baptized Catholics is indissoluble, that is, there can be no true divorce of husband from wife. They may live separately, but they remain married to each other for life. Also, because marriage is a communion of life and love, in order to accomplish the purpose of marriage a man cannot have more than one wife; polygamy therefore is contrary to the law of God.

Jesus raised marriage, which is a natural covenant between a man and a woman, to the level of a sacrament. This means that it is a holy state of life and confers special graces on the couple to enable them to fulfill the duties of married life. Jesus' presence at the wedding feast of Cana, which he blessed by changing over one hundred gallons of water into wine, is a sign of his will to elevate marriage to a sacrament.

A key text in the Bible on the sacramental nature of marriage is found in Saint Paul's letter to the Ephesians, chapter 5, verses 21–33. This text is often read at nuptial Masses. There Saint Paul says that the husband is to love his wife and sacrifice for her, and that the wife is to obey her husband because he is the head of the family. Paul adds an analogy: the union between husband and wife is an image of the love that Jesus, the Bridegroom, has for the Church, which is his Bride, and that love is everlasting. Regarding this similarity the apostle says, "This is a great mystery, and I mean in reference to Christ and the Church" (Eph 5:32). In the Latin text the word for "mystery" here is *sacramentum*. So it could also be translated into English as "this is a great sacrament".

The most important event in the history of the world was the Incarnation of the Son of God in the womb of the Virgin Mary. The Old Testament and the history of Israel were preparations for the Incarnation: God himself became a man; he assumed a human nature in the womb of the Virgin Mary and became one of us; he is our brother in the flesh. The purpose of the Incarnation is to save us from our sins, to redeem us, to make it possible for us to attain the face-to-face vision of God in heaven. Jesus came into this world to do the will of his Father, as he says often in the Gospels. Here is just one example: "I have come down from heaven, not to do my own will, but the will of him who sent me; and this is the will of him who sent me, that I should lose nothing of all that he has given me, but raise it up at the last day" (Jn 6:38–39).

The point to reflect on here is that God became a child in a human family. He lived thirty years in a family situation in Nazareth of Galilee with his parents—Mary, his Mother, and Joseph, his foster father. Jesus spent thirty years in family life and only about three years in preaching the good news of salvation and establishing his Church on the twelve apostles. So God put his personal stamp of approval on family life. He allowed himself to be nurtured, trained, and educated by two of his own creatures—his earthly parents, Mary and Joseph. Jesus' life itself, therefore, is proof enough that God blesses the family and desires that children grow up in a family.

Reflecting on this great truth, Pope John Paul II in his 1981 apostolic exhortation "The Role of the Christian Family in the Modern World" (in Latin, *Familiaris Consortio*) says that the hidden life of Jesus in the Holy Family at Nazareth is "the prototype and example for all Christian families" (no. 86). That apostolic exhortation summarized the results of the 1980 Roman Synod of Bishops on the topic of the family. It is God's will, therefore, that the Christian family should exist and flourish in imitation of the Holy Family as a communion of persons and a communion of life and love.

A final point I would like to make regarding the Christian family is that it is an image of the Holy Trinity. The Trinity is the most basic of all the mysteries in the Catholic faith, including the Incarnation and divine grace. The Trinity is a communion of Persons—Father, Son, and Holy Spirit. There is only one God, but the inner life of God is tri-personal—one God and three Persons. We know this by the divine revelation of Jesus Christ, who speaks often in the Gospels about his Father and the Holy Spirit. The three names are not synonyms for just one Person; they are three distinct Persons, but not separate. This is clearly stated by Jesus in his commission to the apostles at the end of Matthew's Gospel: "All authority in heaven and on earth has been given to me. Go therefore and make disciples of all nations, baptizing them in the name of the Father and of the Son and of the Holy Spirit, teaching them to observe all that I have commanded you;

and behold, I am with you always, to the close of the age" (28:18–20).

The Trinity is a profound mystery that cannot be comprehended by the created intellect, either angelic or human. Saint John tells us that God is love—love is his nature (1 Jn 4:16). The inner life of God is a loving communion of persons—and there is generation and procession, since the Father generates the Son, and the Father and Son spirate or breathe forth the Holy Spirit. So the Christian family, with father and mother who generate children, is a faint image of the inner life of God in the Holy Trinity, where there is generation and a multiplicity of persons. In a certain sense, therefore, the Christian family is a reflection of the inner life of God and helps us to understand in some way the nature of the triune God, whom we worship and serve. From all the above, it is evident that the family exists and has great dignity because it is willed by God, and because the Second Person of the Blessed Trinity in his human nature spent thirty years honoring it.

20

The State and the Will of God

Look on my affliction and deliver me,
  for I do not forget your *law*.
Plead my cause and redeem me;
  give me life according to your *promise*!
Salvation is far from the wicked,
  for they do not seek your *statutes*.
Great is your mercy, O LORD;
  give me life according to your *justice*.
Many are my persecutors and my adversaries,
  but I do not swerve from your *testimonies*.
I look at the faithless with disgust,
  because they do not keep your *commands*.
Consider how I love your *precepts*!
  Preserve my life according to your steadfast love.
The sum of your word is truth;
  and every one of your righteous *ordinances* endures
    forever.

—Psalm 119:153–60 XX (*Resh*)

The state or political community in which we live is a natural society that is willed by God, who is the author of nature. Therefore it has a limited moral authority that must be respected and obeyed. Man is by nature a social being, having been created that way by God. As a social being, he has to live in society with other human persons in order to reach the full development of his personality. Individual persons need many things that they cannot produce themselves. Therefore the tasks must be divided up so that experts in various fields can supply things for others, such as food, drink, housing, education, recreation, and so forth. The individual cannot do all those things for himself.

As we now know it, the state is an independent, sovereign political community that occupies a certain territory with boundaries, such as Canada or the United States of America. It includes the people who live there, who usually are bound together by a common culture and language, and who are governed by a definite constitutional or legal order administered by legitimate authorities, such as a king or president or legislature of some kind.

The purpose of the state is to achieve the common good of all its citizens. Vatican II says on this point: "The political community, then, exists for the common good; this is its full justification and meaning and the source of its specific and basic right to exist." The Council goes on to say in the same place that "the political community and public authority are based on human nature, and therefore that they need belong to an order established by God." [1] So it

---

[1] *Lumen Gentium*, no. 74.

is Catholic teaching that the state is a natural society and therefore willed by God.

Catholic teaching on the nature of the state stresses that its purpose is to provide for "the common good". What is that? Here is the definition given by Vatican II, reflecting the teaching of Pope Pius XII: "The common good embraces the sum total of all those conditions of social life which enable individuals, families, and organizations to achieve complete and efficacious fulfillment." [2] Pope John XXIII said in this context: "The attainment of the common good is the sole reason for the existence of civil authorities." [3]

In this context it should be remembered that the Catholic Church does not favor any one type of legitimate state—kingdom, republic, oligarchy, democracy. Whatever the form, it must obey the natural law and respect the dignity of the human person, who is not a mere pawn in the hands of the all-powerful secular state. At the same time it should be noted that the Catholic Church is opposed to all forms of totalitarianism that violate the dignity of the human person and put themselves in the place of God, such as Nazi Germany, the former Soviet Union, and communist China.

In order to achieve its purpose the state must be able to command certain acts or forbid them. In order

[2] Pius XII, Encyclical on the Unity of Human Society, *Summi Pontificatus* (1939), no. 59; quoted in ibid.

[3] John XXIII, Encyclical on Establishing Universal Peace, *Pacem in Terris* (1963), no. 54.

to command or forbid, the state must be endowed with authority that is recognized by its citizens. Since God wills the existence of the state, for the good of man, and since the state cannot function without some authority over its citizens, it follows that the authority of the state comes from God. Thus, in reply to Pontius Pilate's question to Jesus, "Do you not know that I have power to release you, and power to crucify you?" Jesus replied: "You would have no power over me unless it had been given you from above" (Jn 19:10–11). Jesus thereby indicates the divine source of authority, even though that authority exists in a pagan state such as the Roman Empire.

On another occasion, when Jesus was asked about paying taxes, he said: "[R]ender to Caesar the things that are Caesar's, and to God the things that are God's" (Lk 20:25). Saint Paul told the Romans that they were conscience-bound to obey the secular authorities in the passage that begins with the words: "Let every person be subject to the governing authorities. For there is no authority except from God, and those that exist have been instituted by God" (Rom 13:1). Saint Peter says the same thing: "Be subject for the Lord's sake to every human institution, whether it be to the emperor as supreme, or to governors sent by him to punish those who do wrong and to praise those who do right" (1 Pet 2:13–14).

I would like to point out that authority is moral power over the will of another—a power that can direct another either to do something or to refrain from something.

Since it is a "moral" power over a person's free will, it is or can be binding in conscience. Since all authority comes from God, as Saint Paul says, there is something sacred about it, and so both those who exercise it and those who are subject to it should treat it with respect.

Political or governmental authority, however, is limited. It is limited first of all by the natural law so that immoral laws, that is, laws contrary to the natural law, such as laws that violate basic human rights like abortion and euthanasia, must be opposed. Think of the many Roman martyrs in the early centuries who died because they refused to offer sacrifice to pagan gods or to the Roman emperor. Governing authority is also limited by the state constitution or the legal or traditional rules of a given society.

Those who possess civil authority must govern justly. State officials are obliged to use their authority for the common good and to promote justice in all their activities. This means that they must provide for the general welfare, avert harm as much as possible, avoid favoritism, and refrain from taking bribes. Elected officials such as congressmen must participate in the deliberations of the government, and they must vote against evil legislation. In our day this becomes very urgent, since Catholic legislators are duty-bound to oppose such things as abortion, fetal stem cell research, same-sex marriage, and physician-assisted suicide.

Since the state is a natural society willed by God, citizens have a moral obligation to love their country, to be sincerely interested in its welfare, and to obey its lawful authority. A person who plots against his own country or rebels against its legitimate government can be guilty of a great sin against God and neighbor. Of course, citizens also have the right to defend themselves against tyranny when there is no other way to secure the exercise of their fundamental human rights.

Citizens should exercise their right to vote. Voting in some cases could be a matter of serious obligation if the common good of the state, religion, or the innocent lives of others were involved. In the late 1940s Pope Pius XII urged everyone in Italy to vote in order to prevent a communist takeover of the country.

Citizens as well as aliens should obey the law of paying just taxes in order to contribute their fair share to the lawful expenses of good government and public security. On the other hand, state officials have an obligation not to waste taxpayers' money on useless, dishonest, or extravagant programs.

Citizens are also obliged to help their country wage a just war of defense. They must serve in the armed forces if the government commands them to do so, unless they are convinced from adequate and unquestionable evidence that the war is unjust. Regarding the duties of citizens the *Catechism of the Catholic Church* states: "Submission to authority and co-responsibility for the common good make it morally obligatory to pay taxes, to exercise the right to vote, and to defend one's country." [4]

[4] *CCC* 2240.

We must remember that the state exists for the common good of all and not for the good of government officials or their friends. A state may not infringe on the natural human rights of individuals or families, which they have from God and not from the state. If a government commands citizens to violate the law of God they must refuse to obey, heeding the words of Saint Peter and the apostles to the Jewish officials of the time: "We must obey God rather than men" (Acts 5:29). On this point the *Catechism* says: "The citizen is obliged in conscience not to follow the directives of civil authorities when they are contrary to the demands of the moral order, to the fundamental rights of persons or the teachings of the Gospel." [5]

There is a close relationship between church and state since they both have authority over the same persons. The church has to do with spiritual realities and eternal salvation after death; the state has to do with temporal affairs and the welfare of its citizens during their lives. Two areas where both church and state have a responsibility are marriage and the education of children. Here are areas where conflicts can and do occur, especially if the state claims complete control over both marriage and education. The two authorities actually complement each other, since their purposes, for the most part, are different. In theory there should be no conflict, but in reality there often is. For example, most countries in Europe require

[5] *CCC* 2242.

civil marriage and do not recognize church marriages as valid; therefore Catholics must first get married by a civil authority and then they go to the Church for the sacrament of matrimony.

In addition the state must recognize the freedom of religion on the part of its citizens as a natural, God-given right. On this important point Vatican II said: "The Vatican Council declares that the human person has a right to religious freedom. Freedom of this kind means that all men should be immune from coercion on the part of individuals, social groups and every human power so that, within due limits, nobody is forced to act against his convictions in religious matters in private or in public, alone or in association with others."[6] In the same place the Council goes on to say that the right to religious freedom "must be given such recognition in the constitutional order of society as will make it a civil right."

Both the state and the church are concerned with the welfare and personal fulfillment of its members. A happy and peaceful accord exists between them when the state does not interfere in the internal workings of the church, and when the church stays out of politics. Several popes and Vatican II have stated repeatedly that the Catholic Church has no mandate from God in the areas of politics and economics. The Church does not favor any one political system or economic

---

[6] Vatican II, Declaration on Religious Liberty, *Dignitatis Humanae* (1965), no. 1.

system, provided that they recognize and protect basic human rights and human dignity.

God himself founded the Catholic Church, and he has preserved it for almost two thousand years. The state or civil society is a requirement of man's social nature, which was given to him by God. Therefore the state is natural to man and willed by God. Both societies are perfect in the sense that they have all the means they need in order to achieve the purpose God intended for them. When they work together and respect each other, they promote the common good, personal well-being, and human fulfillment of all their members.

21

Mary and Joseph and the Will of God

Princes persecute me without cause,
    but my heart stands in awe of your *words*.
I rejoice at your *word*
    like one who finds great spoil.
I hate and abhor falsehood,
    but I love your *law*.
Seven times a day I praise you
    for your righteous *ordinances*.
Great peace have those who love your *law*;
    nothing can make them stumble.
I hope for your salvation, O LORD,
    and I do your *commandments*.
My soul keeps your *testimonies*;
    I love them exceedingly.
I keep your *precepts* and *testimonies*,
    for all my ways are before you.

—Psalm 119:161–68 XXI (*Shin*)

In this chapter we will reflect on how Mary and Joseph, guided by divine providence and assisted by the abundant and special grace of God, fulfilled the will of God in their lives. They were chosen and predestined from all eternity to be the Mother and foster father of

Jesus in his human nature—Jesus, the incarnate Word of God, the Second Person of the Blessed Trinity, the Messiah and Savior of the world. First we will consider Joseph, and then Mary of Nazareth, who by the will of God became the Mother of God.

The prophets had predicted that the Messiah would be a descendant of King David. In order to show that Jesus fulfilled that prophecy, Matthew (1:1–16) and Luke (3:23–38) give the genealogy of Joseph, showing that he was descended from David. Since Joseph is the foster father and legal father of Jesus, it follows that Jesus is descended from David. The Gospels do not say whether or not Mary's father was of the family of David, but he probably was, so that Jesus was related to David also through his mother. In the Gospels one of the titles given to Jesus is that he is "the Son of David".

In Matthew and Luke we learn that Joseph was the husband of Mary. How that was arranged we do not know, but it was certainly a result of divine providence. Joseph is an essential part of the divine plan to work out the salvation of mankind by the Incarnation of the Son of God. He was prepared by special graces from his childhood to be the virginal spouse of the Mother of God and to be the guardian, supporter, and protector of the Child Jesus until he reached maturity. As the husband of Mary and the "reputed" father of Jesus, he made it possible for Mary, the Virgin Mother, to appear to others as a normal mother, and Jesus as the son of his married parents. Without Joseph,

Mary and Jesus would have been social outcasts. In his public life Jesus was occasionally referred to as "the son of Joseph".

In the first two chapters of Matthew and Luke, Joseph is portrayed as a "just" man. "Just" in this sense means that he was a holy man who faithfully observed the rules of the Jewish religion of the time. When Joseph learns that Mary is pregnant while she is still living with her parents and has not yet come to live with him, he has doubts about what to do. Joseph is directed by an angel of the Lord in a dream to retain Mary as his wife. This is a manifestation of God's will for him, and he obeys immediately. Later, an angel of the Lord again appears to him in a dream telling him to take the Child and his Mother to Egypt, which he does; when Herod dies, he is again directed by an angel of the Lord to return to the land of Israel. In all of these unusual and miraculous events Joseph obeyed God without any questioning. Joseph is an obedient man of silence. The Gospels do not record any words of Joseph—not a single word.

As the husband of Mary, Joseph was the head of the family, so both Mary and Jesus were under his authority. What a responsibility he had to nurture and protect the Savior of the world and the Mother of God! Joseph is outstanding for his obedience to the will of God, for his humility, for his fidelity, for his love in providing for Jesus and Mary in trying circumstances, especially as a foreigner in Egypt for a year or two when Jesus was an infant.

The New Testament does not say anything about the death of Joseph, but it probably occurred before Jesus entered into his public life. Also Joseph does not appear in the public life of Jesus. His last appearance is when he and Mary find Jesus, at the age of twelve, in the temple listening to the teachers and asking them questions (Lk 2:41–51). An indication of Joseph's early death is that Jesus entrusted his mother to the apostle John when he said to him from the Cross, "Behold, your mother!" If Joseph were still alive, it would not be necessary to entrust her to John, who was not a blood relative.

There is a pious tradition that Joseph died in the arms of Jesus and Mary. Perhaps that is why the Church has named him the patron of a happy death. Pope Pius IX named Saint Joseph the patron of the Universal Church.

Because of his close physical and personal association with Jesus, the God-man, and with Mary, the Mother of God, Saint Joseph is the greatest saint of the Church after the Blessed Mary, who was his wife and companion for almost thirty years. Holding Jesus in his arms and looking into his penetrating eyes, Joseph was intimately close to God, who is the source of all holiness. Therefore he was supremely holy, which means that he embraced God's will in all his thoughts, words, and deeds. Because of his close association with Jesus and Mary, Saint Joseph is recognized by the Church as a powerful intercessor for those who pray to him.

To be holy means to do the will of God. The more perfectly one does the will of God, the more perfect he is. Saint Thomas Aquinas said that the closer one is to a principle, the more he shares in the efficacy of that principle. For example, the closer one stands to a blazing fire, the warmer one becomes. The Blessed Virgin Mary, from the Annunciation to the birth of Jesus, carried the Son of God physically in her womb for nine months. Also she conceived him in her mind and heart before she conceived him in her body. Therefore she was closer to God than any other creature, including the angels. To prepare her for this unique role in the history of salvation, God predestined her from all eternity to be his holy Mother. Accordingly, she was given the special privilege of being conceived without original sin and being "full of grace" from the first moment of her conception and creation. Being full of grace means that she possessed the virtues of faith, hope, and charity to a very high degree, and also that she was endowed with the Seven Gifts of the Holy Spirit. Thus Mary was so endowed with grace and virtue that she was not able to sin; she was impeccable. That is why she is referred to as the "immaculate" Mother of God. She was never touched by concupiscence and sin. God's grace protected her since she was predestined to be the first tabernacle of Jesus' sacred humanity; she was the true Temple of God.

Mary, however, was a free person; she was not an automaton or a passive recipient of God's gifts. Mary actively cooperated in the divine plan of redemption when she uttered her *fiat*, her Yes to God's invitation to become the Mother of God. Thus, she freely consented to be the Mother of the Savior.

Saint Luke records the event for us in his Gospel account (1:26–38). There we read that the angel Gabriel was sent by God to Mary to announce to her that she was chosen to be the Mother of God. Mary raises the difficulty of her virginity and how that could be reconciled with motherhood. The angel tells her that "[t]he Holy Spirit will come upon you and the power of the Most High will overshadow you; therefore the child to be born will be called holy, the Son of God" (Lk 1:35). As soon as Mary understands what God is asking of her she freely assents to his will and utters the words that changed the whole course of human history: "Behold, I am the handmaid of the Lord; let it be done to me according to your word" (Lk 1:38).

When reflecting on Mary's Yes to God, it is important to remember that our Creator does nothing in vain; everything he does is perfect. Accordingly, God made man free. He did not have to create man free, but that is what he did. Also, God respects his own creation. This means that he deals with his creation according to the laws or norms he put into it.

Through the angel Gabriel, then, God approaches the holy Virgin and announces to her that she has been chosen to be the Mother of the Messiah. But the divine maternity is not forced on Mary, for the Annunciation is also a request from God that she give

her free consent. Being a woman of deep faith, in
loving obedience Mary utters her decisive *fiat*.

From the greeting of the angel Gabriel, we know
that Mary possessed the fullness of grace. Thus, the
Holy Spirit was already present within her and with
his grace enabled her to speak her Yes to God freely.
If God had not assisted her interiorly with his grace,
she could not have responded to him with faith and
love. God's grace elevates and assists our powers of
mind and will; it does not cancel them out. Rather, it
goes right along with them, raising them to a higher
level. This is especially true with regard to Mary's Yes
to God. Please note this: God's grace enabled Mary to
consent to God's offer that she become the Mother of
God, and it enabled her to give her consent *freely*.

Mary, therefore, was not a passive agent in the drama
of redemption; she was highly active. Saint Augustine
said that Mary conceived "Christ in her mind before
she conceived him in her womb," that is, she freely
consented to God's will that she be the Mother of
God.

Similar statements about Mary's faith and love
abound in the writings and sermons of the Fathers of
the Church and in the documents of the Magisterium. Thus, Saint Irenaeus in the second century said
that Mary "being obedient, became the cause of salvation for herself and for the whole human race." He
also said: "The knot of Eve's disobedience was untied
by Mary's obedience: what the virgin Eve bound
through her disbelief, Mary loosened by her faith."

Comparing Mary with Eve, the Fathers call her "Mother of the living", and frequently claim "death through Eve, life through Mary."

Referring to Mary's consent to God's holy will, Vatican II said: "The Father of mercies willed that the Incarnation should be preceded by assent on the part of the predestined mother, so that just as a woman had a share in bringing about death, so also a woman should contribute to life."[1] Again, commenting on Mary's *fiat*, the Council said:

> Thus the daughter of Adam, Mary, consenting to the word of God, became the Mother of Jesus. Committing herself wholeheartedly and impeded by no sin to God's saving will, she devoted herself totally, as a handmaid of the Lord, to the person and work of her Son, under and with him, serving the mystery of redemption, by the grace of Almighty God. Rightly, therefore, the Fathers see Mary not merely as passively engaged by God, but as freely cooperating in the work of man's salvation through faith and obedience.[2]

Mary is a type and model of the Church. She has already realized in herself the fullness of faith, hope, charity, and obedience to the will of God that should characterize the Church, which is the Bride of Christ, the Bridegroom. She is preeminently a model of faith because she believed God when he told her, through

[1] *Lumen Gentium*, no. 56.
[2] Ibid.

the angel Gabriel, that she would be a virgin Mother
of the Messiah. She is an example of the "obedience
of faith" that Saint Paul praises in Romans 1:5. Vatican II stressed the same point: "As St. Ambrose taught,
the Mother of God is a type of the Church in the
order of faith, charity, and perfect union with Christ.
For in the mystery of the Church, which is itself rightly
called mother and virgin, the Blessed Virgin stands
out in eminent and singular fashion as exemplar both
of virgin and mother." [3]

When Mary's older cousin Elizabeth greeted her,
Elizabeth was filled with the Holy Spirit: "Blessed
are you among women, and blessed is the fruit of
your womb! . . . For behold, when the voice of your
greeting came to my ears, the babe in my womb
leaped for joy. And blessed is she who believed that
there would be a fulfillment of what was spoken to
her from the Lord" (Lk 1:42–45). In response to that
Mary, inspired by the Holy Spirit, utters her great
prayer called the "Magnificat". Included in that wonderful prayer, sung every day in the liturgy of the
Church, are the words, "For behold, henceforth all
generations will call me blessed; for he who is mighty
has done great things for me, and holy is his name"
(Lk 1:48–49).

Because of her faith, love, and obedience Mary can
rightly be called "the first Christian". Because of her
fullness of grace, she can be said to be "perfectly

[3] Ibid., no. 63.

redeemed".[4] Because of Mary's obedience of faith to the divine will she became the Mother of God and the holiest person God ever created. Saint Catherine of Siena said of her: "You are the first temple of the Blessed Trinity, the first adorer of the Incarnate Word, the first tabernacle of his sacred humanity."[5]

Mary and Joseph attained a very high level of holiness, above all the other saints, because they always did the will of our heavenly Father. Mary had the fullness of grace from the moment of her creation in the womb of her mother, Saint Anne. On the psychological level of personal awareness this means that, from the moment she had the use of reason as a child, Mary was constantly aware of God and always lived in his presence. Accordingly, I think we can safely say that she lived her whole life in what Saint Teresa of Avila refers to as the "mystical marriage" with God.

Because of Mary's fullness of grace, her perfection in virtue, her gifts of the Holy Spirit—and because she is the Mother of God—Saint Bernard, author of the prayer the Memorare, said that we can never say enough about our Blessed Mother or praise her too highly.

[4] Karl Rahner, S.J., *Spiritual Exercises* (New York: Herder & Herder, 1965), p. 263.

[5] Gabriel of St. Mary Magdalen, O.C.D., *Divine Intimacy* (Rockford, Ill.: Tan Books, 1996), p. 42.

22

Jesus and the Will of God

Let my cry come before you, O LORD,
    give me understanding according to your *word*!
Let my supplication come before you;
    deliver me according to your *word*.
My lips will pour forth praise
    that you teach me your *statutes*.
My tongue will sing of your *word*,
    for all your *commandments* are right.
Let your hand be ready to help me,
    for I have chosen your *precepts*.
I long for your salvation, O LORD,
    and your *law* is my delight.
Let my soul live, that I may praise you,
    and let your *ordinances* help me.
I have gone astray like a lost sheep; seek your servant,
    for I do not forget your *commandments*.

—Psalm 119:169–76 XXII (*Tav*)

Jesus Christ, the Son of God, the Second Person of the Blessed Trinity, came into this world of time and space to do the will of his Father. The will of his Father was that he assume a human nature, just like ours, preach the gospel, establish his Church on Peter

and the apostles, and then suffer, die, and rise again
in glory in reparation for the sins of mankind. By so
doing, through his infinite merits, he would confer
on those who believe in him the grace of God that
makes us new creatures, children of God, and heirs
of heaven if we persevere and die in the state of
sanctifying grace. Reflecting on this truth Saint Paul
says in Hebrews 10:5–7, "When Christ came into
the world, he said . . . 'Behold, I have come to do
your will, O God.' "

The entire life of Jesus, from his childhood to his death
on the Cross, was dedicated to accomplishing the will
of his heavenly Father, to obeying all his commandments. When Jesus was twelve years old he left his parents for three days to spend the time in the temple. When
Mary and Joseph finally found him and asked him why
he had done that, he replied, "How is it that you sought
me? Did you not know that I must be in my Father's
house?" (Lk 2:49). Jesus at age twelve was doing the will
of his heavenly Father, which took precedence over the
will of his earthly parents. Saint Luke tells us that they
did not understand what he said to them. Jesus was gen-
tly reminding them that the will of his heavenly Father
came first in his life. But then Luke tells us immediately that the Child Jesus "went down with them and
came to Nazareth, and was obedient to them" (2:51)
because it was his Father's will that he be subject to them
until he reached adulthood.

Jesus' obedience to the will of his Father is a pattern of his whole life on earth. On Easter Monday,

after his Resurrection from the dead, Jesus walked with two disciples on the road to Emmaus and explained the Scriptures to them—how the prophecies all pointed to himself as the Messiah. Then he summarized his whole life as the obedient servant of God when he said to them, "O foolish men, and slow of heart to believe all that the prophets have spoken! Was it not necessary that the Christ should suffer these things and enter into his glory?" (Lk 24:26).

When his disciples asked Jesus to teach them how to pray he taught them the Our Father, which contains the key phrase that sums up the whole prayer, "Thy will be done on earth as it is in heaven" (Mt 6:10).

Again and again in the four Gospels Jesus says that he does the will of his Father. For living human beings, food is essential to maintain life. When Jesus was speaking to the Samaritan woman at Jacob's Well, the disciples asked him if he would like some food; Jesus answers them by saying, "'I have food to eat of which you do not know.' So the disciples said to one another, 'Has anyone brought him food?' Jesus said to them, 'My food is to do the will of him who sent me, and to accomplish his work'" (Jn 4:34). On another occasion, in response to those who were trying to trap him with tricky questions, Jesus said, "'[H]e who sent me is with me; he has not left me alone, for I always do what is pleasing to him.' As he spoke thus, many believed in him" (Jn 8:29–30).

In the quotes above Jesus speaks about being "sent". The Father sent him into the world on a mission to save mankind. In fulfilling that mission of being sent, Jesus carries out the will of his Father. The Gospels, especially Saint John's, stress this notion of Jesus being sent. "I have come down from heaven, not to do my own will, but the will of him who sent me; and this is the will of him who sent me, that I should lose nothing of all that he has given me, but raise it up at the last day" (Jn 6:38–39). Again, "My teaching is not mine, but his who sent me" (Jn 7:16). "My food is to do the will of him who sent me" (Jn 4:34). Jesus' whole reason for coming into this world is to carry out the will of his heavenly Father, who sent him, and that will is the salvation of those who believe in him.

In order to enter into Jesus' kingdom it is not sufficient to respond to his call with friendly words. His invitation must be responded to with faith and love. Near the end of the Sermon on the Mount, Jesus warns us about mere words without the corresponding faith and love that manifest themselves in deeds: "Not everyone who says to me, 'Lord, Lord,' shall enter the kingdom of heaven, but he who does the will of my Father who is in heaven" (Mt 7:21).

As Christians we must always remember that Jesus Christ is not just a holy man and a great moral teacher of sublime truths. Jesus is the Word of God; he is the Second Person of the Blessed Trinity; he is God in the flesh as a member of our human race and therefore our brother. Jesus is the God-man, that is, he has two natures—he has a divine nature and a human nature, but the Person in him is the Word, the Second Person in the Trinity who unites the two natures in his one Divine Person. Jesus of Nazareth has been referred to as the *abbreviated* Word of God. This means that only a small part of the reality of Jesus Christ is made known to us in his human nature because his divinity is hidden for the most part. In his earthly life we get a glimpse of it in his miracles, his Transfiguration on Mount Tabor, and his Resurrection.

When Jesus speaks about his "hour" he is referring to his Father's will that he die on the Cross for the salvation of the world. When his "hour" approaches he takes Peter, James, and John with him into the Garden of Gethsemane, where he prays to his Father for strength to endure the suffering and death that will soon be imposed on him. He repeats his prayer three times: "My Father, if it be possible, let his chalice pass from me; nevertheless, not as I will, but as you will" (Mt 26:39, 42, 44). Another translation renders the Greek in a memorable expression: "not my will, but thine be done." Here we see the distinction between the natural abhorrence of Jesus' human nature to the suffering and death he is soon to undergo, manifested by his human will, and his affirmation and acceptance of the divine will of his heavenly Father, which is also his divine will since he and the Father are one. Here it is important to remember that Jesus, unlike us, has two wills, a divine will and a human will, because he has two natures. His human will obeys the divine will in all things; that is why he can say that he always does what is pleasing to his Father in heaven.

Another aspect of Jesus obeying his Father has to do with the commandments he has received from him. On several occasions he makes reference to this. Thus, he said to his disciples at the Last Supper, "I do as the Father has commanded me, so that the world may know that I love the Father" (Jn 14:31). Again, "[T]he Father who sent me has himself given me commandment what to say and what to speak. And I know that his commandment is eternal life. What I say, therefore, I say as the Father has bidden me" (Jn 12:49–50). "If you keep my commandments, you will abide in my love, just as I have kept my Father's commandments and abide in his love" (Jn 15:10). That Jesus kept the commandment of his Father and that he was totally obedient to him in all things is stressed by Saint Paul when he says of Jesus in the lofty hymn in his Letter to the Philippians: "And being found in human form he humbled himself and became obedient unto death, even death on a cross" (2:8).

Note the connection between keeping God's commandments and having love for him. One who truly loves another is always ready to do his will. "He who has my commandments and keeps them, he it is who loves me; and he who loves me will be loved by my Father, and I will love him and manifest myself to him" (Jn 14:21).

Those who believe in Jesus and love and obey him become members of his family. On one occasion, when Jesus was busy preaching the good news to a large gathering, his Mother and his brethren stood outside the house and asked to speak to him. But he replied, "'Who is my mother, and who are my brethren?' And stretching out his hand toward his disciples, he said, 'Here are my mother and my brethren! For whoever does the will of my Father in heaven is my brother, and sister, and mother'" (Mt 12:46–50). Of course, his Mother was outstanding in doing the will of God, so this is not a rebuke to her. But he does insist that doing the will of his Father is more important than mere blood relationship because it establishes a spiritual bond between him and the faithful disciples who are closely related to him like a brother, sister, or mother.

In the Bible, "justice" is a key concept. It has a much broader meaning than giving to another what is due to him. It means rendering to God what is due to him and being of one will with God. Other words for the same concept are "holiness" and "perfection". It is God's will that we should be holy. Jesus stated this principle clearly in the Sermon on the Mount when he said to the crowd, "You, therefore, must be perfect, as your heavenly Father is perfect" (Mt 5:48). Saint Joseph is called a "just" man, that is, a holy man who was obedient to God in all things. Jesus is the "just" man *par excellence*! He, the absolutely sinless one, in humility went to John the Baptist in the Jordan River and asked to be baptized. When John hesitated and said that Jesus should instead baptize him, Jesus said, "Let it be so now; for thus it is fitting for us to fulfil all righteousness" (Mt 3:15). "Righteousness" here is a synonym for "justice". The justice involved here is God's will for Jesus. One of the Beatitudes is that those are blessed who hunger and thirst for justice, that is, holiness. According to the Bible that holiness consists in conformity to the will of God. Since Jesus' human will is totally conformed to the will of God, he is therefore the absolutely holy one. Because the Baptist knew this about Jesus, he wanted to be baptized by Jesus.

Jesus is the one who perfectly conformed himself to the will of God. After the Bible, for the past six hundred years, the most popular and most read book of Catholic spirituality is *The Imitation of Christ.* The major purpose of the author is to lead others to follow Christ, to imitate Christ, to become another incarnation of Christ by being obedient to God and by doing his will in all things. Saint Ignatius of Loyola often read passages from the *Imitation* and incorporated many of its insights into the constitutions and rule for the Jesuit order, which he founded.

Saint Ignatius offered his entire will to the heavenly Father through Christ in a beautiful prayer that many Catholics say after having attended Mass and received Holy Communion. Please note that the first part of himself that he offers to God is his will, or liberty. This prayer is an appropriate conclusion to these theological reflections on the will of God:

Take, O Lord, all my liberty, receive my memory, my understanding, and my whole will. All that I am and all that I have come to me from Thy bounty; I give it all back to Thee, and surrender it all to the guidance of Thy holy Will. Give me Thy Love and Thy Grace; with these I am rich enough and ask for nothing more.

BIBLIOGRAPHY

Aquinas, Thomas. *Summa Theologica*. 5 vols. Westminster, Md.: Christian Classics, 1981.

Aumann, Jordan, O.P. *Spiritual Theology*. Huntington, Ind.: Our Sunday Visitor, 1980.

Baker, Kenneth, S.J. *Fundamentals of Catholicism*. 3 vols. San Francisco: Ignatius Press, 1982.

Catechism of the Catholic Church. St. Paul's/Libreria Editrice Vaticana, 1994.

Catechism of the Council of Trent. Fort Collins, Colo.: Roman Catholic Books.

Catholic Encyclopedia. New York: McGraw-Hill, 1967.

De Caussade, J. P., S.J. *Self-Abandonment to Divine Providence*. Rockford, Ill.: Tan Books, 1987.

Denzinger-Schönmetzer. *Enchiridion Symbolorum*. Freiburg in Breisgau: Herder, 1965.

De Sales, Francis. *Treatise on the Love of God*. Rockford, Ill.: Tan Books, 1997.

——. *Finding God's Will for You*. Manchester, N.H.: Sophia Institute Press, 1998.

Flannery, Austin, O.P., ed. *Vatican Council II: The Conciliar and Post Conciliar Documents*. Northport, N.Y.: Costello, 1975.

Gabriel of St. Mary Magdalen, O.C.D. *Divine Intimacy*. Rockford, Ill.: Tan Books, 1996.

Garrigou-Lagrange, Reginald, O.P. *The Three Ages of the Interior Life*. Vol. 2. Rockford, Ill.: Tan Books, 1948.

Guardini, Romano. *The Lord*. Washington, D.C.: Regnery, 2009.

Hardon, John A., S.J. *Modern Catholic Dictionary*. New York: Doubleday, 1980.

Kempis, Thomas à. *The Imitation of Christ*.

Leon-Dufour, Xavier, S.J., ed. *Dictionary of Biblical Theology*. Translated from the French by P. Joseph Cahill, S.J. Rome, Italy: Desclee Co., 1967.

Marmion, Columba. *Christ, the Life of the Soul*. Bethesda, Md.: Zaccheus Press, 2005.

McGarrigle, Francis J., S.J. *My Father's Will*. Milwaukee, Wis.: The Bruce Publishing Company, 1944.

Ott, Ludwig. *Fundamentals of Catholic Dogma*. Rockford, Ill.: Tan Books, 1974.

Perrin, Joseph-Marie, O.P. *The Little Manual of Perfect Prayer & Adoration*. Manchester, N.H.: Sophia Institute Press, 2002.

Philippe, Jacques. *In the School of the Holy Spirit*. Princeton, N.J.: Scepter Press, 2007.

Puhl, Louis J., S.J. *The Spiritual Exercises of St. Ignatius*. Chicago: Loyola Press, 1952.

Scanlon, Michael, T.O.R. *What Does God Want?: A Practical Guide to Making Decisions*. Huntington, Ind.: Our Sunday Visitor, 1996.

Tanquerey, Adolphe, S.S. *The Spiritual Life*. Rockford, Ill.: Tan Books, 2000.

The Holy Bible. Revised Standard Version, Second Catholic Edition. San Francisco: Ignatius Press, 2006.